Jakob Kolding

Jakob Kolding   *Shifting Realities*   UMMA Projects 6

Edited by Jacob Proctor
Designed by Jakob Kolding

Photography:
Anders Sune Berg (p. 39)
Edo Kuipers (pp. 49-52)
Fotostudio Paltrinieri (pp. 29, 31, 34/35, 72),
Jacob Proctor (pp. 89, 92)
Lisa Rastl (pp. 43-46)
Adam Reich (pp. 66-71)
Randal Stegmeyer (pp. 90/91)
Antoine Turillon (p. 38)
Jens Ziehe (p. 65)
All other photographs by the artist

Copyediting: Eugenia Bell
Lithography: Licht & Tiefe, Berlin
Printing & Binding: Medialis GmbH, Berlin
Produced in Europe

This publication is part of the artists' books series Christoph Keller Editions published by JRP|Ringier, Zurich.

ISBN 978-3-03764-168-2

Jakob Kolding

Shifting Realities

Christoph Keller Editions

jrp|ringier

Contents

Insert

List of works + Biography/Bibliography

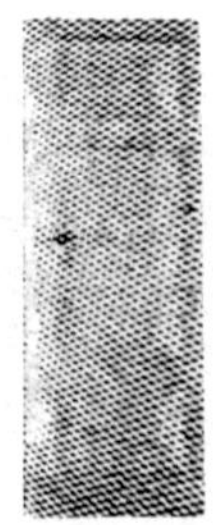

Remixed Use
Jacob Proctor

*"The great obsession of the nineteenth century was, as we know, history…
The present epoch will perhaps be above all the epoch of space."* [1]

— Michel Foucault

1. Michel Foucault, "Of Other Spaces," *Diacritics* 16, 1 (Spring 1986), p. 22.

Since the late 1990s, Jakob Kolding has pursued a sustained investigation of the experience of space in the contemporary built environment. His vantage point is that of a generation born after modernism had already emerged victorious in its battle for cultural dominance, its idealist promises for the future already translated into the inevitable compromises of the present. Yet it is precisely in the relationships and contradictions that emerge in this slippage—between planning and reality, to quote one of his pithier titles—that Kolding finds his inspiration. His collages, drawings, posters, and mixed-media sculptures remix the visual idiom of modernist art and architecture with the subcultural iconography of skateboarding, comic books, sci-fi, and soccer. Where an earlier generation might have seen these as irreconcilable, or at least incompatible, positions in the spectrum between high and low, Kolding thrives on his ability to inhabit a cultural space predicated on the productive potential of such seeming contradictions. Language plays a key role in this process, weaving together dialects as divergent as hip hop and sociology. With an appealing combination of gravity and wit, fragments of lyrics and song titles are deployed alongside academic pronouncements, repurposed as snippets of sociopolitical commentary that paradoxically convey both irony and earnestness.

Kolding's relationship to modernist architecture and city planning has always been an ambivalent one, owing in part to his own experience growing up in a rigidly planned suburb of Copenhagen, a built environment that produced in Kolding both an affection for its modernist architecture and a frustration with its near total lack of flexibility. This ambivalence is crucial to his practice, serving both as its condition of possibility and the object of its analysis. Already in what might be called his first "mature" work—the early series of drawings entitled *Our House* (1997)—Kolding complicated any simplistic equation of architectural standardization with soul-crushing conformity. Rather than decrying their lack of individuality, Kolding instead transformed the uniform façades of his neighborhood into an elegant compositional structure in which the slightest change—in this case in the color of the front door—can have enormous aesthetic impact. (A similar operation occurs in *Stakes is High* (2008), in which the façade of an International Style high-rise is punctuated with individual blocks of color.) Kolding has often played on formal similarities between modular architecture and minimalist sculpture, and here we can see another connection: to the repetitive grooves and metronomic beats of the electronic dance music that has long been an important touchstone for his practice.

Collage has proven to be an exemplary medium for Kolding's investigations in part because it has allowed him to build a vocabulary of recurring forms, each with its own set of cultural resonances, that nonetheless read quite differently as their context shifts from one work to another. From De La Soul to the denizens of the Cabaret Voltaire, from Batman to Buckminster Fuller, repeated figures, motifs, and snippets of text create a visual rhythm and a sense of interconnectedness across a body of work that now spans more than a decade. For Kolding, these subjects are interesting not in isolation but within a context that, like the modern city itself, is the product of a shifting set of interrelations. Beyond the referentiality of any particular element, in Kolding's practice collage both demonstrates the chronic instability of figure and ground and critically reflects the discontinuity of spatial and temporal experience under the conditions of modernity.

In creating his speculative topographies, Kolding draws on early twentieth-century Dada and Constructivist montage techniques, but his aesthetic mode is closer to the sampling and mixing techniques that are the foundation of contemporary hip hop and electronic music. In Kolding's work, collage functions primarily as an additive process; less a means of dismantling an existing order than a way of imagining a new one, built up out of the isolated, defamiliarized fragments of the real. In this way an analogy can perhaps be drawn between Kolding's visual constructions and the cut-and-paste soundscapes of tape music pioneers like Delia Derbyshire. (Most famous for her landmark 1963 electronic realization of the iconic *Doctor Who* theme music, the BBC Radiophonic Workshop composer stars opposite Godzilla and the 1980s minimalist psychedelic rock band Spacemen 3 in Kolding's 2008 collage and drawing *My City*.) Like a producer searching for just the right sample or the perfect break, Kolding mines a kind of cultural unconscious. Familiar images and spaces are made strange through transformations that are both formal and conceptual, gradually shifting our attention from actual space to more amorphous notions of mental or psychological space.

Kolding's work often takes the form of posters that are placed in public spaces and given away to visitors free of charge at exhibitions. In these and other works, Kolding asks questions rather than offering pat solutions. "Have there been any attempts, through planning, to either discourage or promote certain patterns of behaviour in your neighborhood? [Which/How?]" reads an iconic early poster in which a skateboarder uses a sculpture by Robert Morris as an obstacle. In another early work the same text appears above a collage depicting a soccer player heading a ball toward a nondescript row of identical suburban houses. In both cases, the direct mode of address and limited number of collage elements are a necessary function of the posters' temporary positioning in an urban fabric where they must compete for attention with advertising, municipal signage, and graffiti.

In other posters, Kolding employs a more elliptical voice and a more complex interplay of word and image. In the 2010 poster *Untitled (Ann Arbor/Detroit)*, for example, the official-sounding but semantically ambiguous phrase "urban planning and local initiatives" is broken up and arranged like a pinwheel across a nighttime sky, an irregular white line extending down from its center like the stem of a flower, tracing the outline of the work's ostensible protagonist as he turns into the picture plane. Unlike other posters in which the same phrase is followed by questions like "Who is using the space? What is it used for?", here it is left unclear whether the two activities are acting in harmony or discord. Mirroring the work's linguistic ambiguity—and similarly situated somewhere between figure and ground—the white line opens itself up to multiple readings. Is it a force field emanating from the figure, something resistant against which he must push, or—as suggested in another recent work created for the same exhibition—might it represent nothing short of "a flaw in the fabric of reality"?

It is clear that in recent years the agitprop qualities of Kolding's earlier work have given way to a more personal, even romantic, aesthetic. In *Movements* (2008), Kolding exploits collage's capacity to cut across space and time in order to construct a tender moment of continuity between Dada photomontage pioneer Hannah Höch and influential dubstep producer Skream, as tendrils of vinelike vegetation begin to invade the cityscape behind them. This invasion continues in *My City*, spiraling out from the work's center into a pictorial field in which Kolding not only trades pronouns, switching from the third person plural to the personal voice of the first person singular, but also swaps architectures, substituting the functionalism of the International Style for the visionary forms of Archigram.

Ultimately, Kolding's work is concerned with how different kinds of space are defined and how those spaces define how we make our way in the world. Rather than simply cataloguing the countless strategies of spatial regulation at work in the urban fabric or describing social behavior in the context of a given space, Kolding's works encourage us to actively question the relationship between space and behavior, and to imagine forms of self-expression that respond to the world in ways that are both unforeseen and unforeseeable. If our experience of the world conditions the way by which we think about the world, Jakob Kolding would like for us to be able to think the unthinkable.

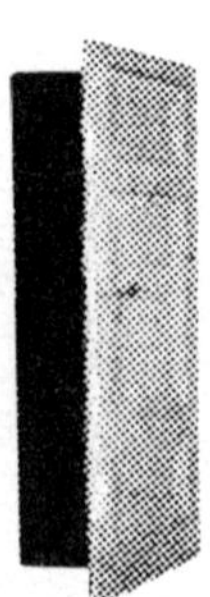

Germs
Lars Bang Larsen

Most folks have left Bellona. Ravaged by riots and fires, its streets are left to the drifters who have come because they have been told that this is where it is at after the Haight-Ashbury scene. What is left of the bourgeoisie is—as usual—painfully trying to keep up appearances, and an aristocratic publisher makes sure that sentences keep circulating in the form of a rudimentary newspaper. People meet at Teddy's, a bar where the beer is free and the entertainment is provided by an energetic male cage dancer. The Kid suffers from amnesia, writes poetry, and leads the Scorpions, a street gang whose cruelty is rivalled only by their laziness. He is of mixed white and Native American origin, and is involved in a three-way relationship with Lanya and Denny, a liaison that is accepted by his otherwise mainly black and straight gang. The two suns that are setting on the entropic urban fabric testifies to the implosion of time. Bellona is a state of being; a vertiginous and giddy condition.

In Samuel Delany's novel *Dhalgren* (1975), time and space are unhinged. It is an apocalyptic text but also one in which language itself is a protagonist, offering resistance to its reading in the way of other great modern novels (no doubt the deserved canonical context for this masterpiece of science fiction). Sometimes the narrative flops into formlessness as it describes an everyday that is no longer ordinary; or the pages decompose into nonsense that makes the reader's own time viscous and heavy. In its narrative structure, *Dhalgren* is deprived of conflicts that conventionally drive a narrative. It is a book that doesn't lose the plot, but deliberately releases it. The Bellona condition is characterized by being post-urban, post-economical, post-desire. There are, in a certain sense, no problems left. Money and class aren't problems, nor is with whom you have sex. Family, race, and politics are no longer issues. The struggles are over. The law is yours. You only need to let go. Subjectivity floats in unmapped configurations of energy.

Jakob Kolding situates his work a little further inside culture than Delany; not after, but perhaps just before civilization breaks down. If things tend toward circularity and plasmatic formlessness in *Dhalgren*, Kolding's point of departure is the forms of existing culture and the ways in which they may be recombined. But he, too, operates in cracks between worlds, where loose ontologies are on the prowl for new confederacies of meaning and new signs to speak through.

Style Wars

Kolding's favored methods are collage and montage. This is a procedure related to the history of experimental filmmaking and avant-garde graphics, as much as to the applied and commercial arts. By removing signs from their referents the artist performs a disruptive gesture that is followed by reconstruction and re-contextualization. Capital's disruption of social connections is appropriated and re-enacted in a dismantling of claims to transparency. No concessions are made to representation and nature. Conflict is embraced and staged without arbitration between surfaces of friction, and through the repeated cross-cutting of the separation of pictorial elements: the cuts can never be healed and the contrasts within the recycled imagery remain tangible. Also the artist's individuality is shown to be under pressure from epistemological shocks and no longer whole or given, incapable of big promises and of producing anything but gaps.

Thus montage is a dialectical method that operates between violence and revalidation, noise and dispersion, self and context. This fundamental ambivalence is the rhythm of Kolding's work, its tension and groove. If equilibrium can be achieved—between elements on the surface of the paper, or in social space—it can never again be a question of unity, but of a synthetic and precarious balance between many parts. Any sublation is necessarily a stitch-up, a permutation.

The visual sources for Kolding's work—the images he breaks open and retools—were in his early work typically derived from historically specific debates on modular architecture. This is the scenario and lasting heritage of a pervasive modernity: in the 1960s, Scandinavian cities such as Copenhagen and Stockholm had some of the worst housing conditions in Europe. To alleviate obsolete housing and derelict neighborhoods, extraordinarily high building targets were adopted, and the satellite cities were built. Much of the housing was completed in a hurry, it was dense and monotonous, and lacked services like transport and recreational facilities, let alone the complexity and details that make up an urban fabric. In some cases, the sattelite towns created a surplus of unlettable dwellings or were stigmatized because they became homes for people who had no other choice.

In Kolding's vision, architecture's apodictic ideologies are undermined. Built space no longer dominates lived space. His work upsets the knee-jerk causality that social housing is the origin of social ills by generating doubt about its ideologies and realities, while never allowing the doubt to petrify. Hence postwar modular urbanism is a heritage that Kolding also pays homage to, for instance by demonstrating how an International Style in architecture—today often represented by ghettos—extends into culturally refined signs, such as Minimalist styles in art and music. Looking back, this modernity does not only seem utopian because its social promises were, in some cases, misconceived on the drawing table, but because the encompassing social vision it represented is rarely attempted.

Such a multifaceted perspective on urbanity gels with agendas of social reform that are inherent to the Constructivist style often employed by Kolding; the agitational aesthetics with slogans, dynamic angles, and floating shapes that has such design-minded artists as Alexander Rodchenko, El Lissitzky, or László Moholy-Nagy in its family tree. Kolding's carving up of architecture on paper as a procedure is as radical as it is delicate, and his formal strategies are generative on their own, not just an infrastructure for content. Most readings of Kolding's work have situated him as an authorial subject in the urban fabric; here he is seen to engage with articulating tensions brought about in meetings between subjectivity, architecture, and urban planning. In his collages, functionalist architecture is tripped up by the specificity of references to fan culture related to music, soccer, and comics. These subcultural indexes relocate the denizens of the global suburban population—not least to themselves. The architecture that they live in may be the same (whether it is in Albertslund, Brasília, or Chicago) but it is colored by their local teams (Brøndby, Brasília, Bears), or by the music they listen to—that may also be picked up over the airwaves by others like themselves, somewhere else. Through these markers, the top-down perspective of a technocratic father figure is scaled down to the needs and desires of lived reality.

Ina Blom discusses how the stylistic binds in Kolding's work move across many different registers at once, and how "(t)he traces of a decidedly artistic style and the stylistic connections to a life-world in which (Kolding) is himself rooted continually bounce off one another because, in visual terms, they seem to be more or less the same."[1] Blom's reading across art, life, and style dismantles dominating postmodern concepts of style; namely a transhistorical architectural gaze constituted

1. Ina Blom, "A Question of Style," in *Momentum II* (Moss: Biennial for Nordic Art, 2000), p. 12.

through a vocabulary of styles available to sample and quote, as well as a post-Marxist critique to which style is bound up with capital's reduction of social space to surface and code. As Blom points out, there is something else entirely at stake in Kolding. Style is neither transhistorical nor a parameter for alienation, but a micro-political stance, a site from which the subject speaks his minor history.

Ultimately, however, Blom's elegant hermeneutics tends to exclude other political concepts. The bone of contention here is the quotations from sociological analyses employed by Kolding as visual/textual fragments in his collages. Here, Blom argues, Kolding "lays bare his weapons":

> A regular feature of the early [modernist] photomontages was the interaction between image and text; in Kolding's case, the brief fragments are immediately recognizable as the clichés of a sociological discourse on the institutional forms of culture and its relation to questions of class. In other words, he makes use of fragments from precisely that discourse through which sub-cultural styles are validated in their essential difference from "official" culture or the art system. And, as fragments, these very recognizable statements on "class," "identity" and "leisure" become just as obliquely devoid of meaning or just as "stylish" as the ubiquitous punk swastika.[2]

2. Ibid.

For one thing, a reading of Kolding that is underpinned by a subcultural concept of style becomes suspect because the visual homogeneity of style—at least in his more recent works—is being unworked and taken apart. Rather, Kolding turns style into a syntax through which not only determined relations between sign and referent are upset, but in which the resulting forms themselves are mixed with a view to constructing a texture of lived experience. Heterogeneous signs and multiple perspectives are picked up by a subject who traces and tests liminal social and symbolic conditions, for instance by coupling a cow with a DJ, a Donald Judd with a housing estate, body with text, image with sound. Kolding's work is not subject to the hygienic operations with which style is otherwise kept clean and whole; the territorial imperative that also subcultures adhere to in their self-expressivity.

In other words, Kolding's work produces lines of flight out of style's gravitational pull of fascination. Sure, the graphic quotes have a propagandistic punch. When a poster reads "Dominio delle spazio e resistenza" or "Get us out of this hell," they may be recognizable or opaque as slogans or discourses—like the chorus of a pop song, a soccer chant, or the collective voice of the political rally—but it is also a call to make sense of our common existence across communities. The punk swastika was threatening not because punks were perceived to be Nazis, but because of the obnoxious ease with which they emptied the swastika of meaning and turned its mythology against straight society. Kolding's gestures of reappropriation are rather more affectionate and concerned, of course, and through his stylistic vocabularies he produces exchanges with the fate of spaces that we share. Thus he isn't kidding when he is employing "sociological cliché" in his work.

Unrealistic in a model–like way
A subcultural style is explicitly and necessarily carried by a body in a life-world. This is the biopower of style, so to speak; the way it is predicated on affect and certain perceptions and behaviors organized around sounds, designs, languages (or even types of food, from the hamburger of the hip-hopper to the lentils of the hippie). The subcultural subject cannot escape its embodiment in contemporary urban and technological space. The *now*—and the entire sociology that envelops it—is its reason for being, for its oppositionality and its pleasure.

Aesthetic experience, on the other hand, is at odds with social and psychological subjectivity. When an attempt is made to transpose aesthetics into life practice, the consequences are usually disastrous, politically and existentially. The singularity and specificity of aesthetic categories of work and author are incommensurate with common and shared conditions such as citizenship and democracy. This postulate may sound conventional. However, one of the critical potentials of aesthetic experience, and its fundamental disparity with instrumental reason, is that we may speculate on the impossibility of subtracting ourselves from the social space of our life world as a way of the status quo. The aesthetic experience nips away at who we already are, displacing us towards future conditions. This is not a matter of reintroducing absolute categories in art, such as media or autonomy, nor of denying the relevance of the visions that art may have for democracy, or refusing a sociology of art's conventions and institutions. Such a subtraction of oneself from social space is in itself present in the aesthetic experience as an active component in the work.

A few examples can help to clarify this. When Kasimir Malevich distilled his pioneering version of abstract art, Suprematism, he claimed to have severed pure feeling in creative art from "the environment in which it is called forth."[3] This is particularly impressive as his "environment" was ravaged by civil war and extreme poverty. There was hardly paint to paint with. Imagine insisting on the supremacy of the non-existing world on an empty stomach! One may call this position fantastic and fanatic, and even callous or stupid; all of this only adds to the sense of crisis and wildness with which one must read the formalism of Malevich. Similarly—to make a comparison that is offbeat in relation to Malevich, but maybe closer to Jakob Kolding—when Sun Ra fantasized about extra-terrestrial life he didn't indulge in escapist fantasies, but articulated Afro-Futurism as a speculative take on race in an attempt to claim the excluded outside as one's own. "There now exists a separate kind of human being," Ra wrote, "the American Black man. And I should say that he doesn't belong on this Earth."[4] In this way, to insist on aesthetic experience as a caesura, as a way of subtracting oneself from the life world without being able to transcend it, doesn't have to eclipse the violence of social space. Aesthetic experience is a threshold of becoming and not eternal, not exalted, not monumental. When it lifts itself out of this world, social space follows it like the tail of the comet; this is art's decentered movement through which it constructs new worlds that are embedded in the situations that make up life.

We may reconsider aesthetic experience in terms of utopia, in Jean Baudrillard's sense of the term as ambivalence and irritation, rather than a homeland or a privileged political space. Utopia is necessarily deferred. Baudrillard writes,

> Utopia is never spoken, never on the agenda, always repressed in the identity of political, historical, logical, dialectical orders. It also haunts and crosses them irrevocably, forcing them into an overstatement of rationality. Utopia does not write itself into the future. It is always, from right now, what the order of the day is missing. [...] Utopia is the ambivalence which crosses every order, every institution, every rationality, even "revolutionary" rationality, every positivity, no matter what, and returns them to their non-place. Utopia is the deconstruction of every unilateral finality of man or history.[5]

Utopia is not a telos, but perhaps aesthetic, or at least compatible with the ambivalence and radical scepticism through which art returns real events to its non-place. Like utopia, art is insoluble and uninhabitable. Its speech is always threatened by reality principles—whether it is economy or some political practice—to which aes-

3. Kasimir Malevich, *The Non-Objective World: The Manifesto of Suprematism* (Mineola, NY: Dover Editions, 2003).

4. Quoted in Debbora Battaglia, "Insiders' Voice in Outerspaces," in Battaglia, ed., *E.T. Culture: Anthropology in Outerspaces* (Durham: Duke University Press, 2005), p. 17.

5. Jean Baudrillard, "Utopia Deferred ..." in, Jean Baudrillard, *Utopie Deferred: Writings from Utopie (1967–1978)* (New York: Semiotext(e), 2006).

thetic experience is a lack, a seductive specter forcing authoritative replies of "overstated rationality" (what is to be done!) and metaphors of presence that are unfaithful to its potential that will always be indirect and symbolic. This is art's rigorous indefiniteness; its politics against the political.

Productive as readings of Kolding's work in terms of style and urbanism may be, there is a line of artistic investigation beyond these (and certainly beyond autobiography too).[6] If earlier pieces employed references that largely coincided with the life span of someone born in the early 1970s, the surfaces of his work are now stratified historically and submitted to anachronistic confrontations, through references to remote pasts and remote futures. Organic growth in the forms of creepers and naked branches have begun a rhizomatic invasion of the pictorial field, introducing timelessness and a threat to the metropolis. Other species assist in breaking down the human body as a fixed and stable category; on their own, or in quasi-mythical mutations between man and bird that defy any binary logic (*Untitled (Zuidas)*, 2010). Kolding has, in other words, begun a deconstruction of the plane of reality. He was always a space jockey, but it is increasingly apparent that his work is lifting off from social and architectural spatialities and urging him to also spin the artistic and imaginary spaces that are involved in productions of reality.

One can refer to this side of his work as its romantic aspect; if only to suggest that it can no longer be read in the vein of *proposals* (analogous to a constructivist or subcultural ethos of art-into-life practice), as it withdraws from analyses of behavior in order to inhabit more speculative and ambivalent terrains. This is nowhere more apparent than in Kolding's "stage sets." These point to a type of enunciation that is different from the collage, namely the model or the miniature. But they are nor models for, or of, something. Made of picture elements and little wooden sticks and placed on podiums or in glass cases, these small sculptures or microinstallations do not claim completeness, thereby thwarting any impulse to create fundamental frameworks for social processes.

Erinnerungen an der Zukunft (2009) is one such combination of collage and sculpture, made for Wien Museum, in Vienna, and based on archival materials related to the museum's construction. As always when the stage sets become visible as such, the division between reality and illusion is blurred. In this way, *Erinnerungen* is a diorama that makes for a museum of the museum, or a play in which the protagonists are the archive, representation and history. The agents that were involved in the building of the museum—the architect, the Austrian president, the mayor of Vienna—dominate the collages. Disturbing elements are naturally also present, represented by a woman—the Dadaist Emmy Hennings, holding a puppet—and the artist himself, photographed from the back, standing inside the museum and looking out at the committee of the museum's founders. As one part of the sculpture, Kolding has placed the mayor in front of an historical statue of an ancient Austrian duchess. This juxtaposition that flips the mayor from being a figure of authority into being a voyeur, or reducing him to being a little boy that is caught looking through the keyhole to the ladies dressing room: the medieval representation of femininity upstages modern man with an oozing sexuality, while the mayor—and the other men in the diorama who are supposed to represent progress and enlightenment—appear rigid and armored in their hats and long coats. (An association: the dissonant simultaneity of picture elements in Kolding's stage sets remind me of Öyvind Fahlström's Pool Paintings from the 1960s: game structures or schizophrenic picture puzzles in which picture elements physically and semiotically collide and create constellations that come about and are dissolved again arbitrarily. In Kolding there is a similar humor and undertow of menace.)

6. If Julian Stallabrass's description of Kolding's work is superficially correct, he misunderstands its critical intent: "Jakob Kolding uses constructivist forms in his collages, pitching old, radical visions of extreme disorientation (as found in the Russian revolutionary avant garde) against the politely regulated architecture and social planning that were its Scandinavian progeny. Kolding was brought up in one of Copenhagen's model suburbs in which everything was safely pedestrianized, and shops, schools, nurseries, and clinics were close to hand. This, we are meant to assume, is a terrible fate, and no doubt must be so until these facilities are closed." It is safe to conclude that Stallabrass's larger, critical project is compromised by shoddy research and biased criticisms at the level of the individual work that fully confuses his own presumptions of suburban life with that of Kolding's suburban space. See: Julian Stallabrass: *Art Incorporated: The Story of Contemporary Art* (Oxford and New York: Oxford University Press, 2004), pp. 52–53.

The toy and the game, Giorgio Agamben writes in his essay "In Playland: Reflections on History and Play" (1978), are "what belonged—once but no longer—to the realm of the sacred or of the practical-economic." This is because toys and games on the one hand contain the residue of sacred rituals from ancient ceremonies and divinatory practices. But toys and games have, on the other hand, a practical-economic model, because they refer to objects which still belong to the realm of utility (a car, a gun, cooking utensils, and so on). Agamben writes:

> What the toy preserves of its sacred or economic model, what survives of this after its dismemberment or miniaturization, is nothing other than the human temporality that was contained therein: its pure historical essence. The toy is a materialization of the historicity contained in objects, extracting it by means of a particular manipulation. While the value and meaning of the antique object and the document are functions of their age—that is, of their making present and rendering tangible a relatively remote past— the toy, dismembering and distorting the past or miniaturizing the present—playing as much on diachrony as on synchrony—makes present and renders tangible human temporality in itself, the pure differential margin between the "once" and "no longer."[7]

7. See also Lars Bang Larsen, *Palle Nielsen's* The Model: *A Model for a Qualitative Society (1968)* (Barcelona: MACBA, 2010).

Miniaturization through play, then, is nothing other than the cipher of history. A model is something paradigmatic, exemplary, a matrix for how things should be. This is the model that internalizes and reproduces the norms and hierarchies whose genesis and structure it displays for the purpose of being replicated and perpetuated in turn. On the other hand, a model can also be something absolute, a counter-image to what exists—even to what can come into existence. It is a draft of what is yet to be, and might never be, because it cannot be realized as itself, outside of itself. A model is in this sense a singularity that inhabits a differential temporal margin. As Kolding's stage sets, the model hovers over the ground of everyday life, bringing on de-realization and ripping up normative social structures that hold down time and space.

When was the future?

Futurity has its own history. Ironically, the future's moment is in many ways behind us now; considering not only the Futurists and other historical avant-garde exercises in ushering in a new world, but also the way that science fiction and comic books embodied an otherness, a different symbolic energy, when the high/low cultural segregation was still in place. This is no doubt symptomatic for our contemporary world. In a globalized world that is often thought to be a totality, with nothing outside of the present order, future imaginaries are in a crisis. We live in a future predicted by a prophetic advertisement on the back of the catalogue for Harald Szeemann's 1967 exhibition *Science Fiction* at Kunsthalle Bern (probably the first in exhibition history that dealt with the subject, and focusing on "the mythology of tomorrow"): the one-page ad for International Business Machines reads: "Science fiction anticipates the future. IBM creates it."[8] Seen from the IBM perspective of cybernetic governance, it is clear how contemporary (un)reality has caught up with sci-fi and annulled its promise of a new, radical modernity. Hence, their point of departure is no longer in a galaxy far, far away, but the irritated materiality of our present world, stuck in time.

8. Harald Szemann, ed., *Science Fiction*, exh. cat., Kunsthalle Bern (1967).

Kolding deliberates the status of futurity accordingly by placing its semiotics in a force field where cultural models for narrating and explaining lived experience may turn out to be inadequate or proven to be contingent. In the words of Debbora

Battaglia, the extraterrestrial is "a foreignness appropriate to lived experience beyond comprehension and our zones of comfort and visibility."[9] By using figures from *Star Wars*, for example, he produces a multidirectional historical pull: Darth Vader hasn't arrived here from the future, but is more likely a childhood memory of the artist. To begin with, such movies are the work of a suburban generation of American directors portraying their own childhood fascination with the Hollywood they absorbed through television. Similarly, when Kolding, in his research, revisits speculation on the future it is probably in the form of literature such as Samuel Delany, or J. G. Ballard and the Strugatsky brothers, or even earlier sources such as Yevgeny Zamyatin's *We* (1921), a novel in the form of a prose poem that evokes a totalitarian society not unlike the Stalinist regime that later censured Zamyatin's work. In other words, science fiction and future imaginaries don't bring us the future, they produce incontrollable historical feedback effects between layers in time.

In the collage *When Was the Future?* (2008), Kolding has combined the sunny skyline of Los Angeles, visible inside the eponymous text, with an image of Dresden. A tree that is so naked and stark that it could have been cast in concrete cuts into the pictorial field from the right; underneath it, a guy is breakdancing on the snowy ledge at the top of a skyscraper. The two cities were, at different times and in different political systems, considered "cities of the future." A title each has lost, like so many other cities across the world that have been similarly predicated. Any future is determined by when, how, and by whom it is conceived. It is a projection on the screen of a present: Kolding's work allows us to see both the structure of the screen and the image projected onto it. In *Memories of the Future* (2009) the point is made in an even more nomadic imaginary that features Hannah Höch and Lewis Caroll's Alice drifting between pictures of student riots in Paris during May 1968 and a photo of a defunct Detroit factory. Industrialization and revolution as mythical futures from the twentieth century, with Höch and Alice as some of the protagonists who were involved in dreaming this modern world. Jean Baudrillard: "Utopia is the smile of the Cheshire cat, the smile that floats in the air before the cat appears and for a time after he disappears. A little before the cat takes his place, a little after he vacates it. This smile annuls the Cheshire cat and is itself mortal."[10]

One of the historical forms for the affirmation of new phases of historical development is the germ. It awaits favorable conditions to develop and find its appointed place, somewhere, sometime. Thus up until the romantic era, thinkers theorized on germs of stars that are scattered in the Milky Way and developing under certain conditions or pressures into comets, which may eventually be attracted into a planetary system. At the beginning of the nineteenth century, the great idealist socialist Charles Fourier departed from the fact that everything is connected in a universal system.[11] There must hence exist a means of communicating between creatures of the other world and this one. The ether–like "aromal fluid," Fourier claimed, was this medium for the great chain of being, a connection between the Earth and the rest of the universe. This aromal fluid is "… a system for the distribution of known or unknown aromas, which control men and animals, form the seeds of winds and epidemics, govern the sexual relations of the planets and provide the seeds of created species."[12]

This means of communication is the supersensible exhalation of the planets: to Fourier, a scientific fact to which the population of the earth must attune their souls in order to achieve interplanetary harmony.

Such a vision of cosmic togetherness is ultimately out of synch with Kolding's tension-ridden work. No holism could survive in the environment of his collages.

9. Battaglia 2005, p. 10 (see note 4).

10. Baudrillard 2006 (see note 5).

11. Emanuel Swedenborg and Charles Fourier, for example. See I. D. Lloyd-Jones, "Charles Fourier: Faithful Pupil of the Enlightenment," in: Peter Gilmour, ed., *Philosophers of the Enlightenment* (Trowbridge: Edinburgh University Press, 1989).

12. Gareth Stedman Jones and Ian Patterson, eds., *Charles Fourier: The Theory of the Four Movements* (Cambridge: Cambridge University Press 2008), p. 16.

But let us stick with the germ and the contact consciousness that pervades his work in an alien key. If the suburb is a condition that is inimical to otherness—even to the passing of time—Kolding's work can be read as the seeds of a plague that is ready to invade all the strata of society's social body and completely disorganize it. This germ is freedom's ambiguous promise, or premise. To Antonin Artaud, the plague offers the body a unique opportunity to get rid of itself; in the same way, Kolding's artistic anti-bodies are let loose on the existing world in order to let other space-times break out on terrains that believe themselves to be immune to change and the sci-fact of difference. This is his internally conflicting surfaces and montaged forms; the physical symptom of Kolding's suburban plague is his site specific practice, in which he distributes large editions of his posters on walls in urban space, like some kind of rash on the skin of the city.

Noise Is Music to His Ears (2008) is a collage and drawing, populated by human and animal. A sparrow sits on the shoulder of a serene looking guy, the musician and DJ Lawrence. Both are perched at the edge of the paper on the background of the grainy image of a grey skyline. The text that runs along the black branches descending from the top of the image stems from two newspaper articles: one about songbirds in urban areas that have begun to sing at night because the urban noise during the daytime prevents them from being heard; the other concerns a man who sought permission—and got it—for building a house between a motorway and a railroad because he was fond of noise. The ways in which sound and city define each other is seen to be absolutely dependent on a subjective position, whether this subject is a bird, a man who likes noise, or a DJ. Noise as a seed—a buzzing germ—awaiting favorable conditions to break out and vibrate ... No doubt these musical noises are significant sounds, maybe like the cosmic hum that overwhelms Carlos Castaneda after having ingested *mescalito* that ensures him psychedelic passage into a crepuscular, psycho-spatial zone:

> *The noise reminded me of a science fiction movie in which a gigantic bee buzzed its wings, coming out of an atomic radiation area. I laughed at the thought.*[13]

Watch the gigantic bee, tune into the disharmony of the spheres, and hear Jakob Kolding laughing too.

13. Carlos Castaneda: *The Teachings of Don Juan: A Yaqui Way of Knowledge* (Berkeley: University of California Press, 1968).

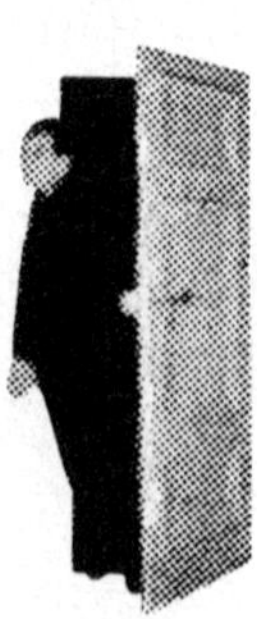

Like Shadows
A Conversation between Jacob Proctor and Jakob Kolding

JP: We've decided to title this book *Shifting Realities*, a phrase that suggests a number of different things in relation to your work. On the one hand, it could refer to the way that your works isolate aspects of the world and recontextualize them, building up a new imaginary world out of all these bits and pieces. On the other, it could speak to the importance of context in your work, particularly the posters, the implications of which can vary quite a bit based on where they are shown.

JK: This title, as you say, touches on many aspects of the works. I guess first and foremost the importance of avoiding *one* "reality" that overrules all other realities, or put differently, other ways of structuring, formulating, and experiencing the world. This, in a very concrete way, translates into how the works, and the single different elements they consist of, never have one stable, finished meaning. By its very nature collage always points to the importance of context and by often reusing the same elements I am interested in building up a kind of shifting vocabulary.

On the importance of context, can you speak a bit about the differences between working and exhibiting in Ann Arbor and Detroit?

I have to admit that I sort of felt like I was on a pilgrimage when I first visited Detroit. I have so much music from there, and I was very excited about seeing the place that all this great music originated in. I felt I had heard so much from the city, read so much about it, that it was so central to me without my ever having been there. A mythic city. At the same time, though, it is clear that many people know Detroit for more negative things. Another myth—and an altogether more negative one—that I, of course, also knew. At first, this actually made it quite difficult to find a way to say something. I did not want to fall into the pitfalls of either confirming that everything is horrible or else coming in from outside and telling everyone how exciting it is that everything has gone wrong. So, for the two posters I did for this show, and which were shown in both cities, I opted for two very open and, in a way, not very specific posters, which seemed to me to be a very specific reaction to this specific context.

It's interesting that in order to make works that responded to a specific context without being "about" that context, you almost had to empty the posters of any really recognizable references.

Yes, exactly. I specifically wanted to work with the geographically very close, but socially and economically very distant cities of Ann Arbor and Detroit, and I wanted the posters to be made equally for both contexts to underline the notion that the works never have one stable reality. Even though the same posters were simultaneously shown in both cities, they could never be quite the same works because the viewing situations were so different. In a way, though, I started with the one thing I felt that both cities had in common: *lots* of parking garages, a feature that also allowed for an indirect link to the dominant industry in the area. So, a nighttime image of a parking garage became the background image of the first poster, but from there on I wanted to leave it very open, so that it could really go in very different directions depending on who would see the poster and where. The point was not to make a work about parking garages, but rather to find a type of space that would be common to everyone, and most likely a space people think about as a space for a practical purpose without reading too much into it, as opposed to more recognizable institutional buildings or clichéd images of factories or abandoned homes. In the end, the change that I made to that space is pretty minimal and, I hope, very open to different interpretations.

That change being this ambiguous, irregular line that connects the two posters to one another formally …

Yes; I actually thought of it as a flower when I started, but it has obvious references to graffiti, as well, or even an accidental doodle. In a way though, it's like a crack in space that, whether by accident or deliberate intervention, can become something potentially productive. In Ann Arbor, as I see it, there are few cracks in space; everything seems very orderly and highly functional. Detroit on the other hand is famously full of cracks: socially, physically, economically, and politically. Although it would be ridiculous to romanticize that situation, in a certain way it does open the door for something new, but what that might be is very hard to tell. In both cities cracks can be understood as the breakdown of a system, either in a negative sense or in a productive sense, as the potential for something other, for new ways of thinking and living to emerge.

As a technique, collage allows for—one might say even encourages—illogical shifts in scale and impossible formal juxtapositions that might echo the kinds of perceptual shifts that can happen when dreaming or under the influence of certain drugs. Do you see either of these as operative in your work? I don't propose to make a psychoanalytic interpretation of your work, but would it be fair to speak of it in relation to a kind of cultural (or subcultural) unconscious?

I think that's a very nice thought. I've always appreciated how with collage you continuously rework established structures by recontextualizing the different elements or by changing the usual order or scale of them. How if, for instance, you make a person bigger than a house, then this change in scale immediately means that you have to look at both parts and their interaction in a completely new way and hopefully not only look, but also think about them in a new way. This works, of course, both in a political sense—I've often tried to work with how this could affect ways of thinking about urban space and how inherent relations of power between, for instance, planner and user could be restructured—but also in a much more ambiguous way, which, precisely as you say, is much closer to what happens in dreams where familiar places, people, or objects suddenly appear "different" in a way that is hard to define.

Do you feel that over the years you've gradually shifted toward this more ambiguous approach, or has it been there all along, perhaps only becoming more apparent over time?

I would say that I've become increasingly interested in a notion of uncertainty in the works, in using doubt and ambiguity as productive forces to destabilize ideas, relationships, and even objects otherwise taken for granted. This interest in an abstract, mental, and psychological space has become more obvious recently, but it has always played an important part in my work. For example, I was never interested in urban space as a static physical space, but always as a process of interrelations, with no way of separating the physical space from the social, psychological, or political space. In a way I feel that the works have broadened from a focus on how a space is planned, how it is being used, and what actions are possible or not possible to a much broader concern with what it is and is not possible to think. Obviously thinking what cannot be thought is a contradiction, but I think that's a nice thing and certainly shouldn't stop one from trying. I have come to appreciate how, for instance, a man upside down can be a comment on power, on the use of space in a very concrete sense, a literal expression of seeing things from a new perspective, or how it can express a kind of existential feeling. It's a thing I love about collage that you can make such notions literal, and I like it a lot when these different ways of seeing start to merge and no one single perspective is clear anymore. This confusion between ways of seeing also leaves space for a lot of humor, which is important. In this way I see my works as sort of temporary propositions rather than successful attempts at world creation. They are in no way complete worlds with any utopian notions.

I wonder if you might talk about the ways that the use of language in your work has changed over the years. Especially in the posters, it seems to me that your use of language has become more oblique or elliptical recently.

I think that in general I've gradually moved away from somewhat didactic sounding texts toward more open or ambiguous phrases. And these days I also often don't include text at all, which was rare earlier on. Previously, I think I was perhaps less confident that the works would be understood without rather direct textual pointers. I used a lot of quotes from social studies or urban planning texts and was interested in taking them very much at face value in terms of where I wanted to go with the work, but at the same time I was also interested in trying to disempower the texts in the context of the work. Unfortunately, a bit too often people would choose either the one reading or the other, fitting the works into easy boxes and seeing them either as pretty dry political statements or, in the opposite direction, seeing them as ironic. In this sense I think that sometimes the works were misunderstood precisely because of the texts. I really wanted to insist on a place where it was possible to do and say multiple things at once without having to choose one reading as the right one, that the "statement" should come from the interference between overlapping systems of meaning more than from any one thing. Lately I have tried to make this position more clear, in part, by either leaving language out of the equation entirely or by choosing much more ambivalent snippets from genres like science fiction, which I really like for its capacity to rethink the world from scratch, at times inventing totally new rules for reality.

It's also interesting how the same kind of language—and here I'm thinking of song lyrics, which have been a more or less constant presence—can take on very different connotations based on what other kinds of text they are juxtaposed with. For example, the phrase "Power, Corruption, and Lies," which you borrowed from the title of a New Order album, reads quite differently in the context of a phrase like "Popular and State Discourses of Power" than it does in the context of a more ambiguous phrase like "Stakes is High" or "When Was the Future?"

That's true, and this was always something I was interested in, to bring this ambiguousness into didactic sounding texts. Funnily, though, I also think the more recent shift in preferences of source material can be illustrated purely in terms of New Order quotes. Whereas earlier I gravitated toward "Power, Corruption, and Lies," which I do still like, I have to say, more recently I used the phrase "Up, Down, Turn Around (oh you've got green eyes, oh you've got blue eyes, oh you've got gray eyes")," from their druggy love song "Temptation," as the title for a work.

Your work obviously incorporates material from all over the cultural spectrum, some of which we've already discussed. I've always thought that this range was valuable not only because it builds up an interesting world for me, but also because it provides a multiplicity of ways into that world, points of access from a variety of positions with respect to different forms of cultural knowledge or literacy. How important is it for people to get the references?

Of course for me, when I work, all the references and all the different elements are very important. So, in that sense they are essential in the process of actually constructing the works, and it's equally important that they are there in the finished work. They are there for a reason and carry a lot of meaning. However, I always try to make the works in a way where the different elements also stand on their own even if you've never come across any of it before, be it a building, a person, a quote, a record cover, an artwork, or whatever. It's important that you can take them at face value so to say. That said, I do hope that there are different points of entry to the works, different ways of navigating them depending on who is viewing and where they are coming from. It's also very important that every element actually opens up the work to something outside itself. In this way it's the opposite of trying to make a work that, when all the elements are added, is finished or complete. Instead the works expand and continue outside themselves. At times I've wondered if I should make more of an effort to let the viewer in on the references. But it's very tricky. If I leave a real list of footnotes, telling where every element of the works come from, I fear that people would stop looking and searching themselves and would instead look at the "fact sheet" for the "correct" solution, which would be totally against the whole point. I think I've come to the conclusion that I'd always be happy to talk about the works if anyone wants to, but otherwise I have to leave it to the viewer and stay out of it.

One clear downside to getting caught up in the footnotes, so to speak, is that you can easily lose sight of the importance of formal issues in how the works function and produce meaning.

The formal side is crucial and there is no way to separate the content from the form since the interplay between the two is what the work is really about. It is also what makes it impossible, I hope, to look at the works to simply decode the "footnotes" for a complete "1 + 1 = 2" understanding. I'd like to make works that make people want to look closer—which is necessary if you really want to see them properly—so that they function in one way when you look at them from a distance and another when you move close. In that way I'd like them to encourage different perspectives in a literal sense. I would also like them to express a sense of openness, whether by actually leaving a large part of the paper empty to suggest incompleteness, or by making works were you don't feel pinned down to one specific way of seeing them. For me, the works are not an explanation but an uncertainty. Although this has always been part of the work I think there has been a change where more recently this has become much more clear and more important to me. It's an important point to bring up the formal side as it often tends to remain a bit in the background when talking about the works.

Of course when it comes to collage and photomontage even formal decisions can become referential to a certain degree …

Yes, and for instance the rather dry aesthetic of some of the earlier works was borrowed primarily from political posters and textbooks. It was an attempt to use the formal vocabulary in a different way and to include elements that would in a way undermine the very reading that the format suggested. However, it brought with it the danger of quick categorizations that would determine how people read the works. I've tried gradually to expand the degree of formal variation in my work, something that has allowed a whole new set of references, meanings, and new ways of seeing the works to emerge. It was always important to me to constantly try and change perspectives and rework everything, over and over, but I feel freer to do that now, whereas earlier I sometimes felt more obliged to do things in a specific way. As with the texts, I think I was afraid of not being clear;

now not being clear is what I aim for. The formal references that you mention are as important as any other references in the works in that they point to something outside the work itself that is nevertheless an integral part of it. I think an important part of working with any kind of found material, be it in visual art, music, film, writing, or whatever is that it underlines the fact that any new creation is, of course, always based in an already existing world and that nothing comes out of nothing.

For a while now you've also been making sculptures that seem to operate somewhere between an architectural model and a stage set. How is the experience with the sculptures different from the posters and collages?

Although you could say that they essentially are collages in three dimensions, I think they bring something very different to the work. In some of the earlier sculptures I would, on site, build a whole structure that looked kind of like a mixture of an architectural model gone wrong and a game of Mikado and then place cut-out figures within that. These loose, open, and very fragile structures were sometimes placed on a sort of podium and sometimes built directly into the space—on a stairway or around a heater, perhaps, so they would incorporate the space in a way that was different from the collages. They were also impossible to move, so they would only exist at a specific place for a specific time and were often so fragile that I had to make running repairs during openings. This fragility was part of the works, as was the idea that they were temporary statements. Lately I have worked with a different type of sculpture in showcases where the showcase itself is very much part of the work. Inside the vitrine there are small tableaux, like stage sets, as you say. In these works I'm interested in exploring the bare minimum that it takes to define a space and suggest a narrative. For example, you might have a situation where, depending on how you see it, a man either leans against a rudimentary building structure or provides the support that keeps the structure from falling. Or one in which a man is just enough out of scale to no longer fit into an architectural structure. These situations suggest a universe, admittedly a very basic one, with action and narratives running through it. So, although they do not move, I actually feel that they involve a sense of action and duration in a way that is different from the collages, and that these three-dimensional scenarios somehow bring a different drama to the work. Humor also plays a very important role here; I like to think of them as simultaneously evoking both stage sets of Samuel Beckett plays and Buster Keaton. I think this existential drama accentuates an aspect of the works that was present before, but far less defined. And by being three-dimensional, you also have to view these works in a different way, and in moving around them you always see the back of the figures as you walk around the work, always there as these suggestive, but abstract shapes. Like shadows.

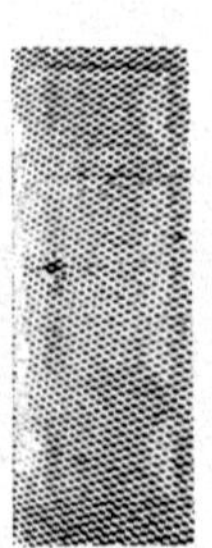

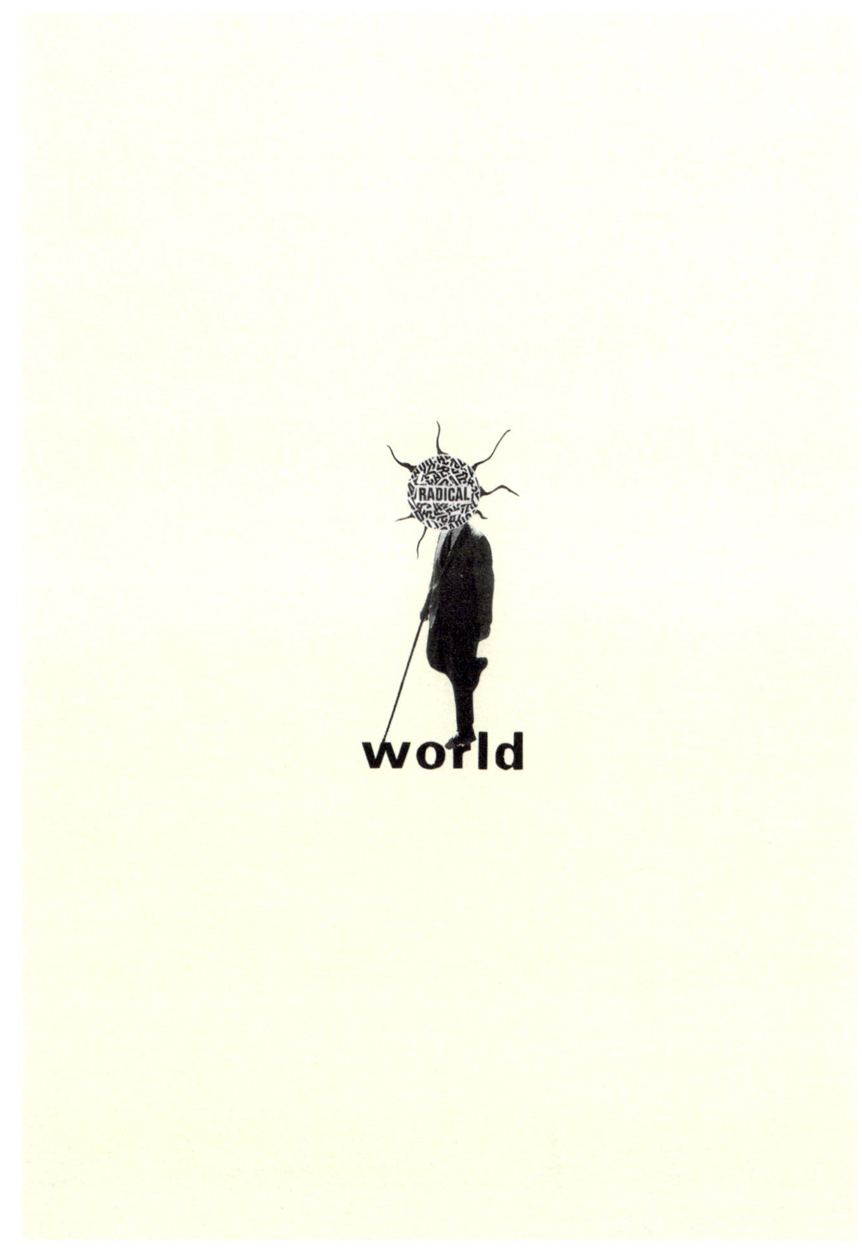

RADICAL
world

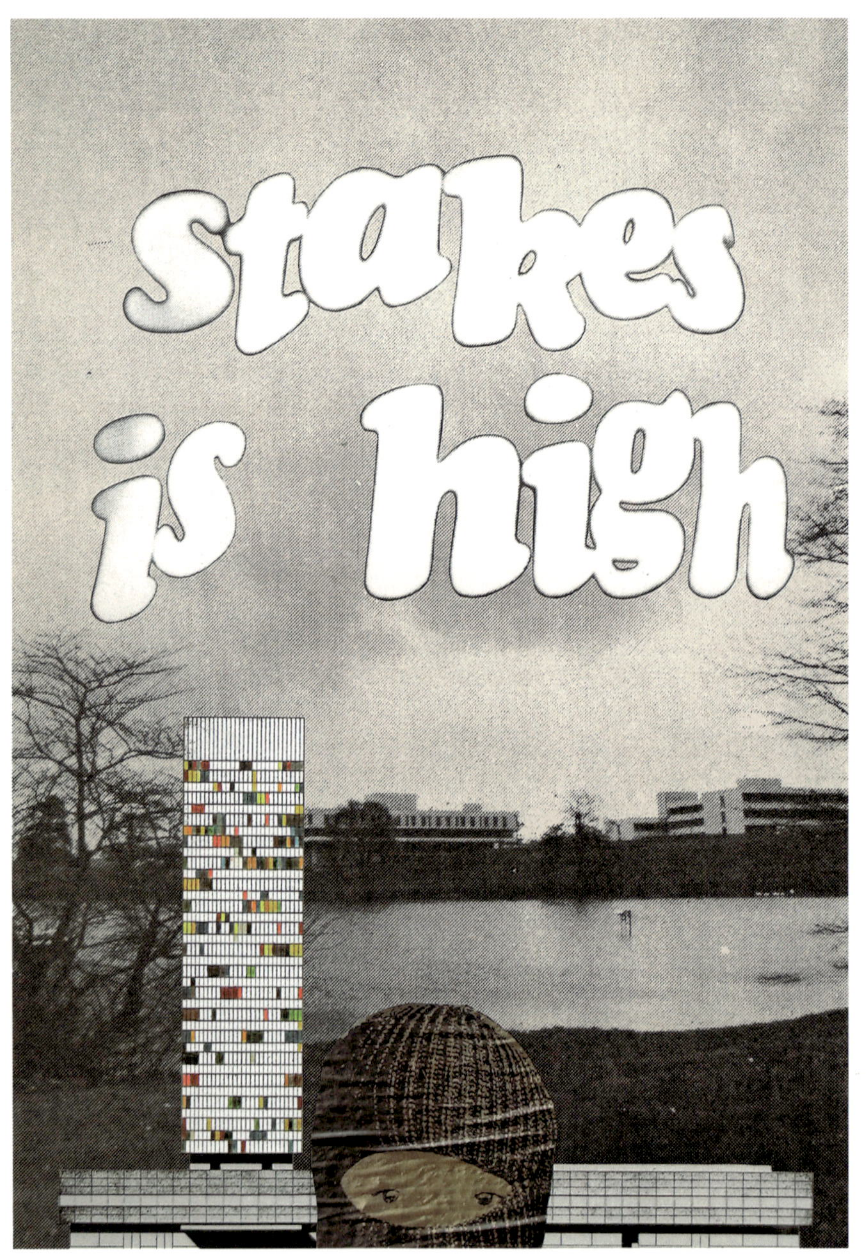

stakes
is high

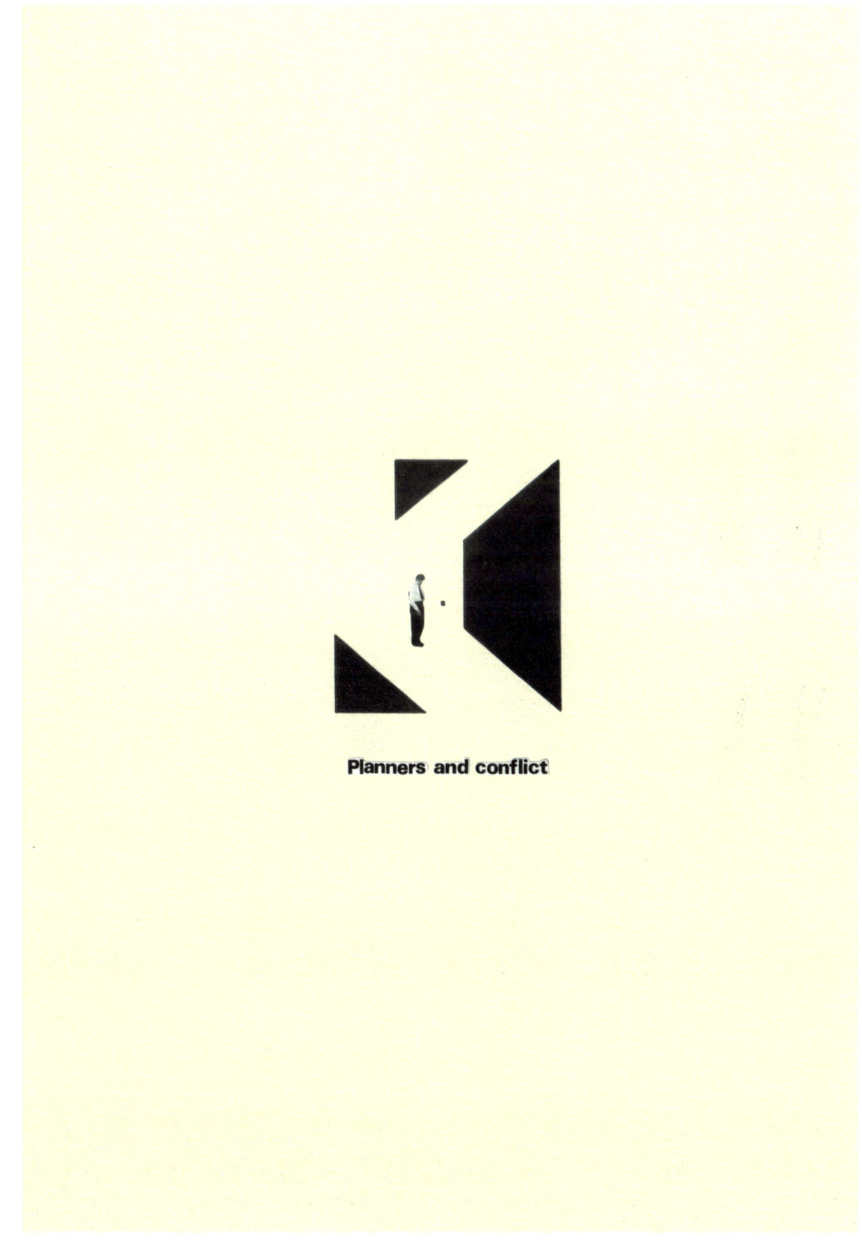

Planners and conflict

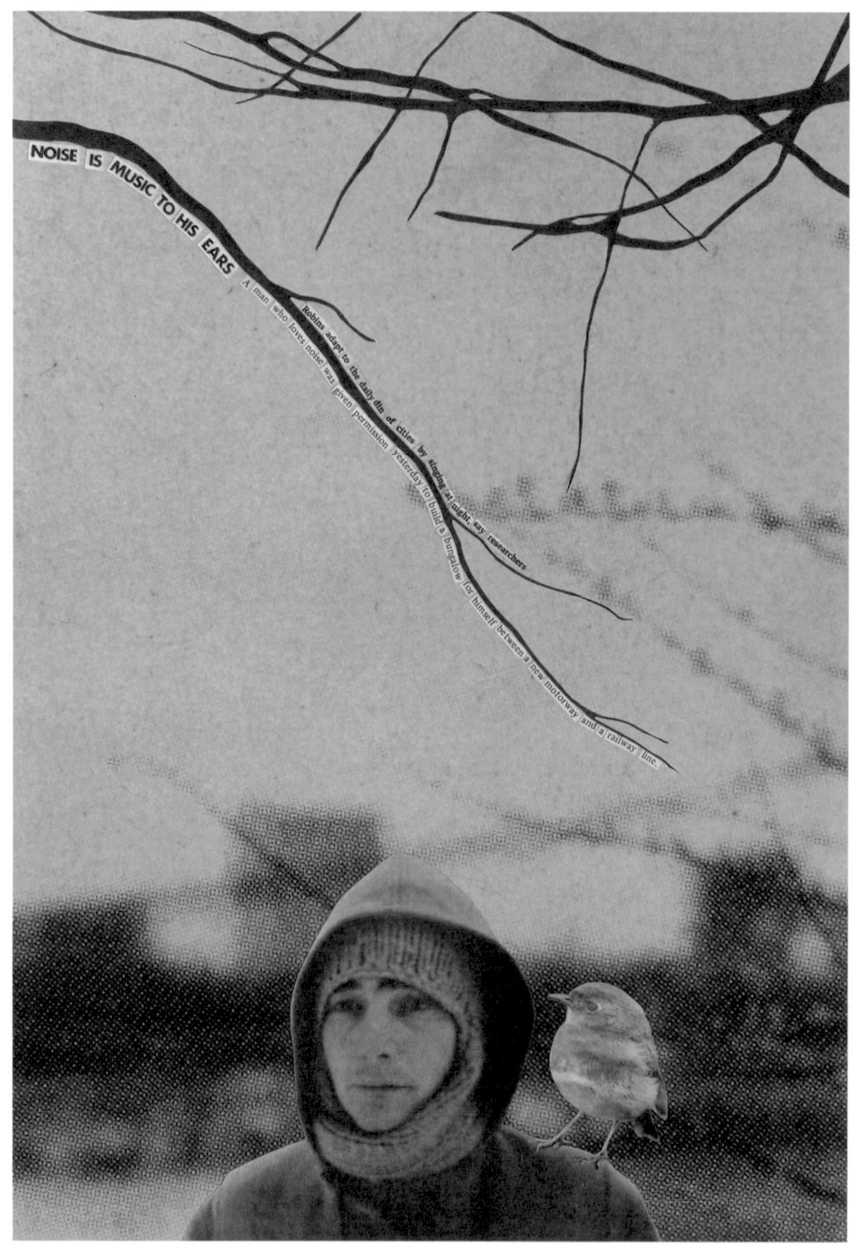

NOISE IS MUSIC TO HIS EARS
A man who loves noise was given permission yesterday to build a bungalow for himself between a new motorway and a railway line.
Robins adapt to the daily din of cities by singing at night, say researchers

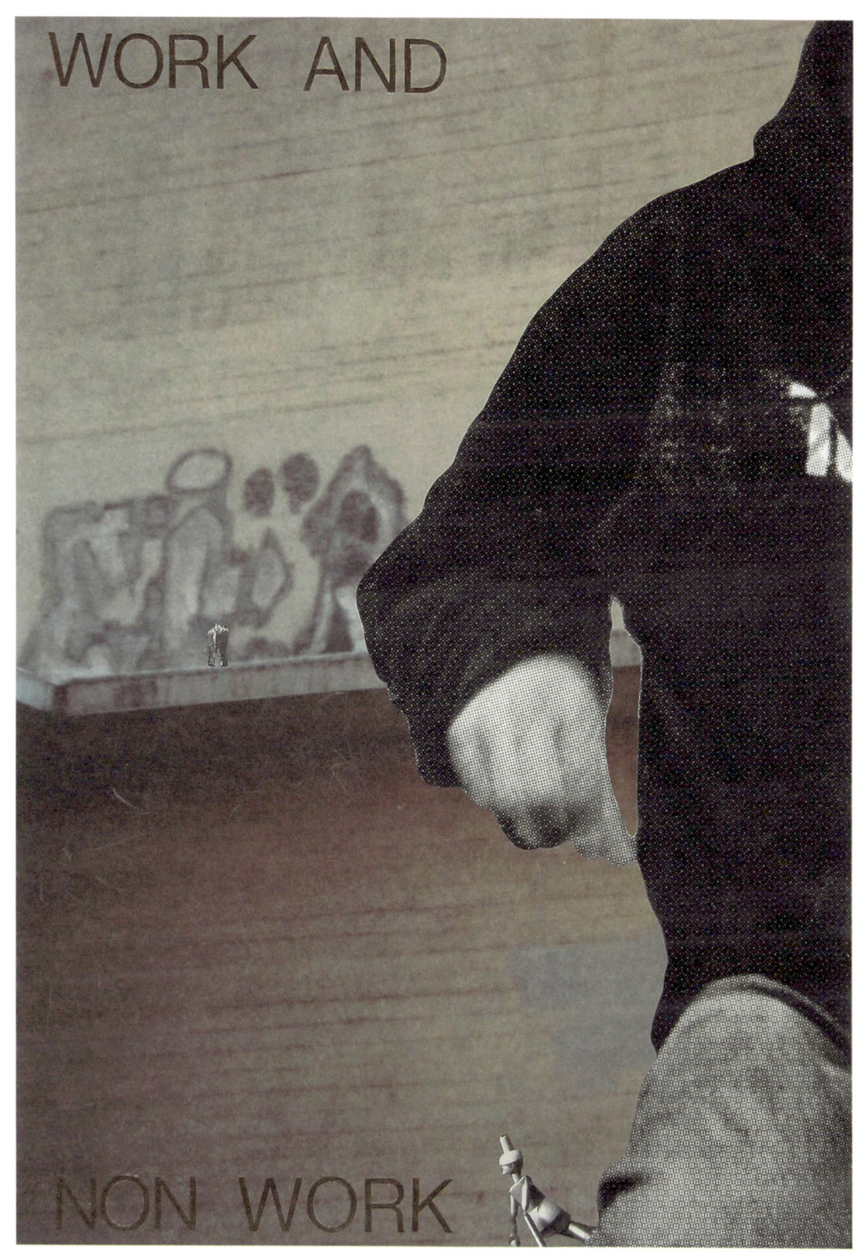

WORK AND
NON WORK

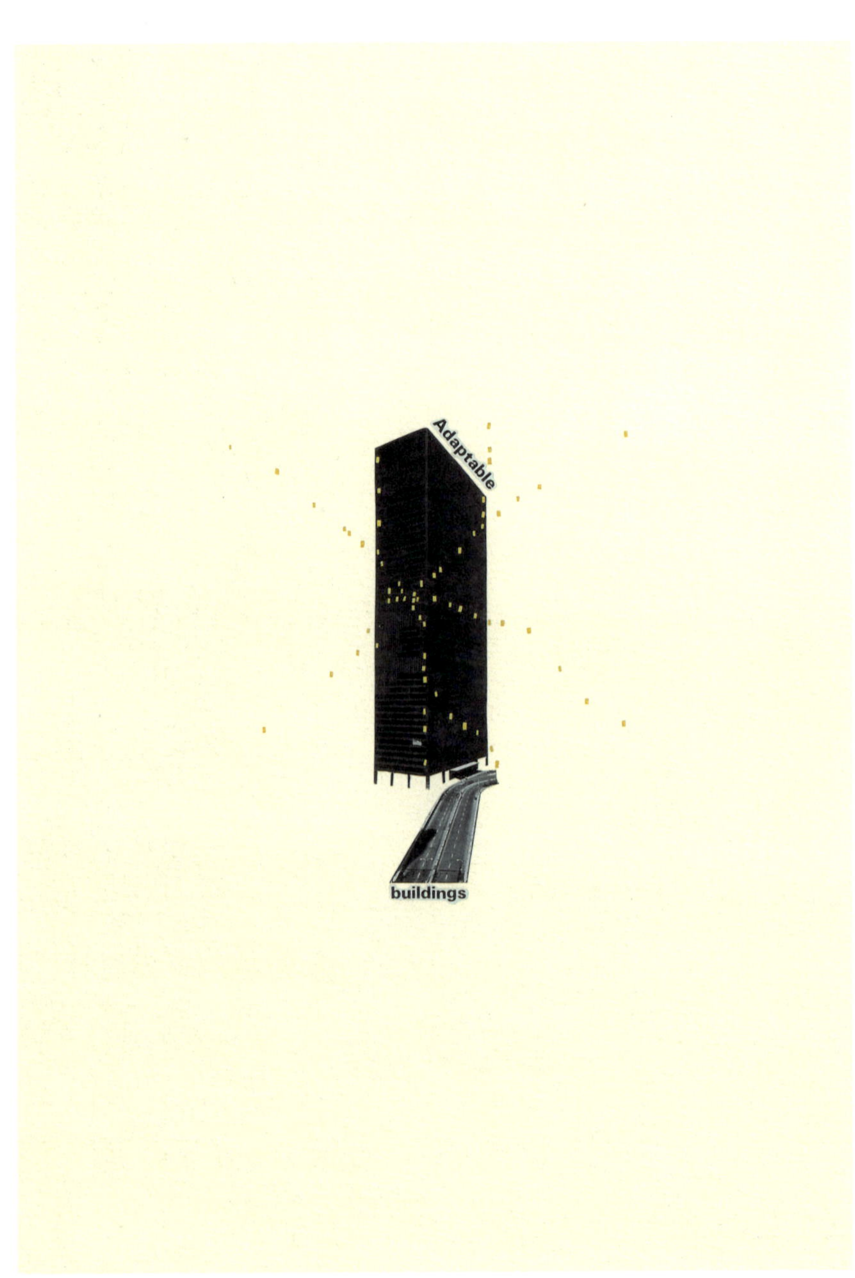
Adaptable
buildings

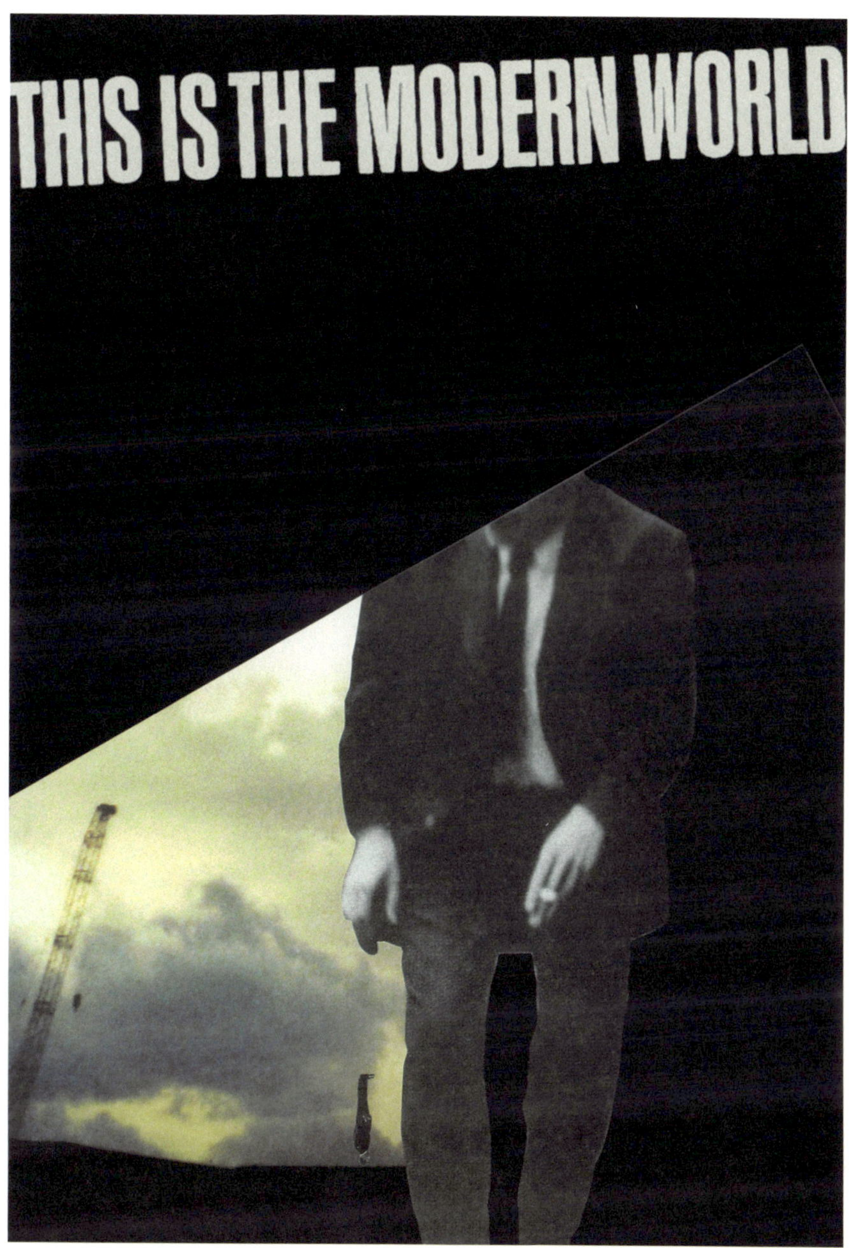
THIS IS THE MODERN WORLD

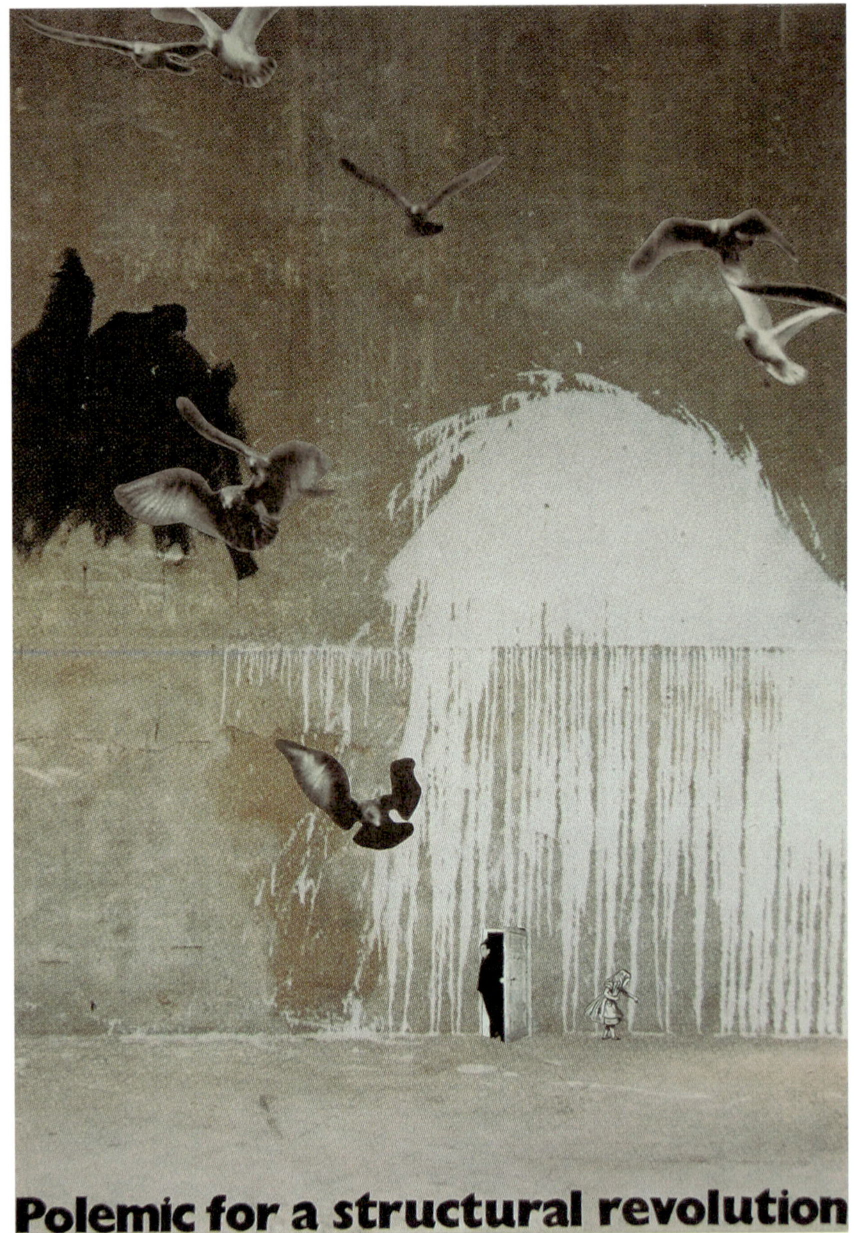

Polemic for a structural revolution

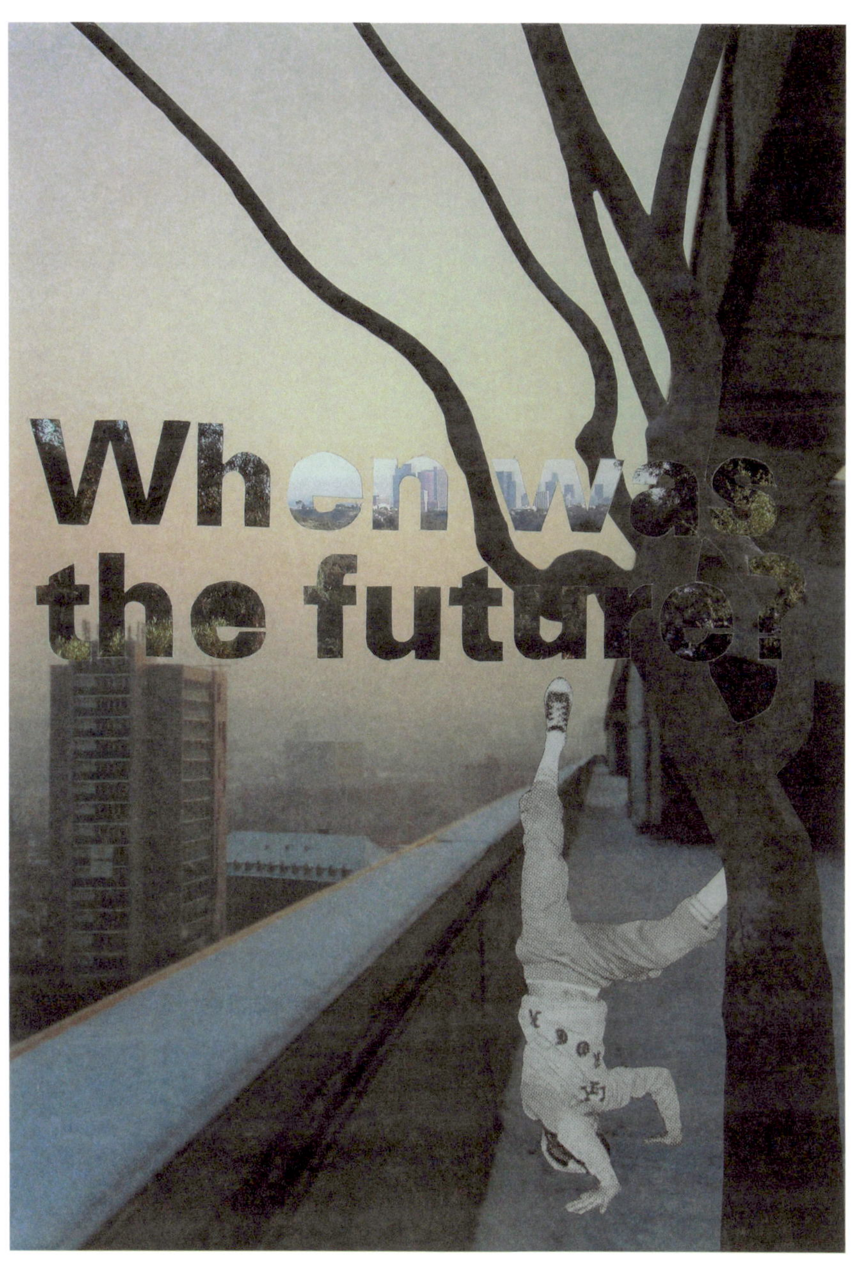

37

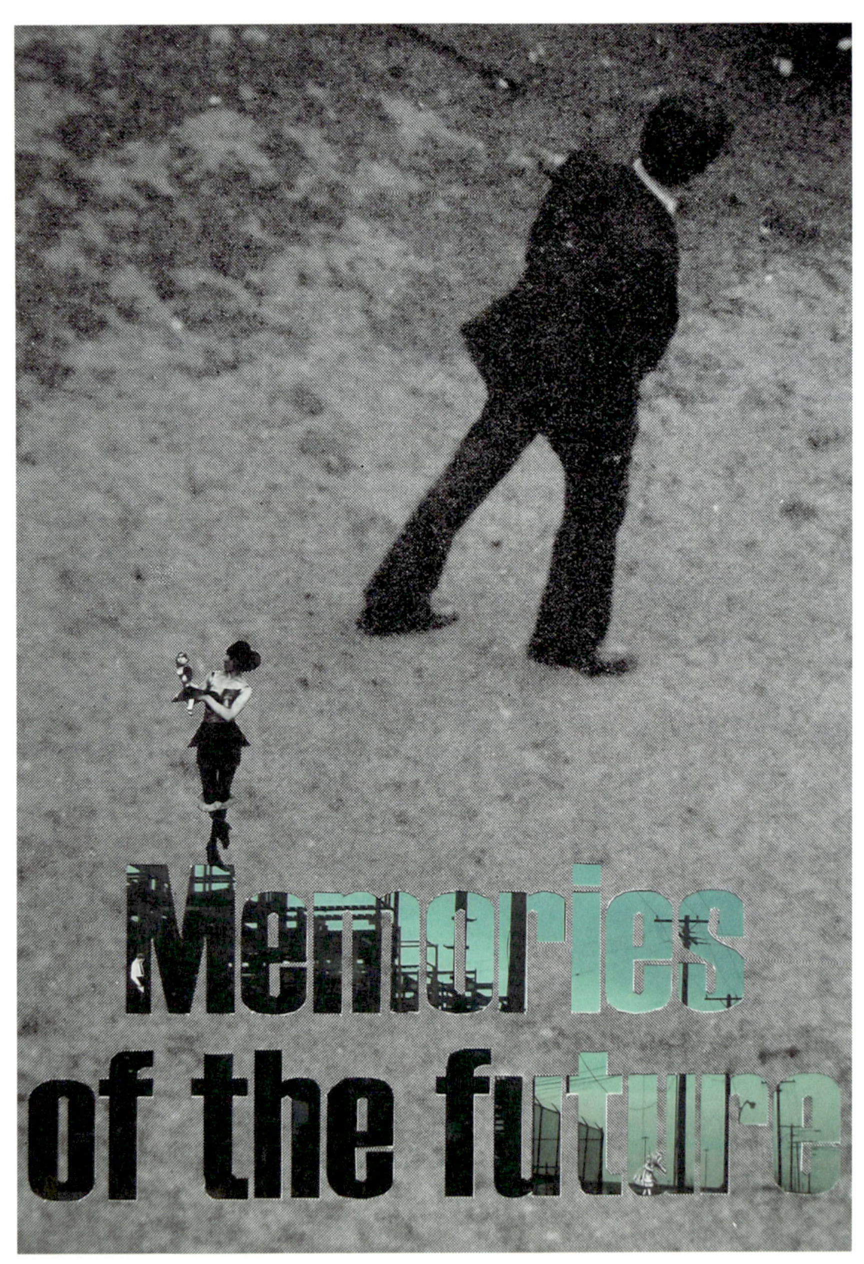

Memories
of the future

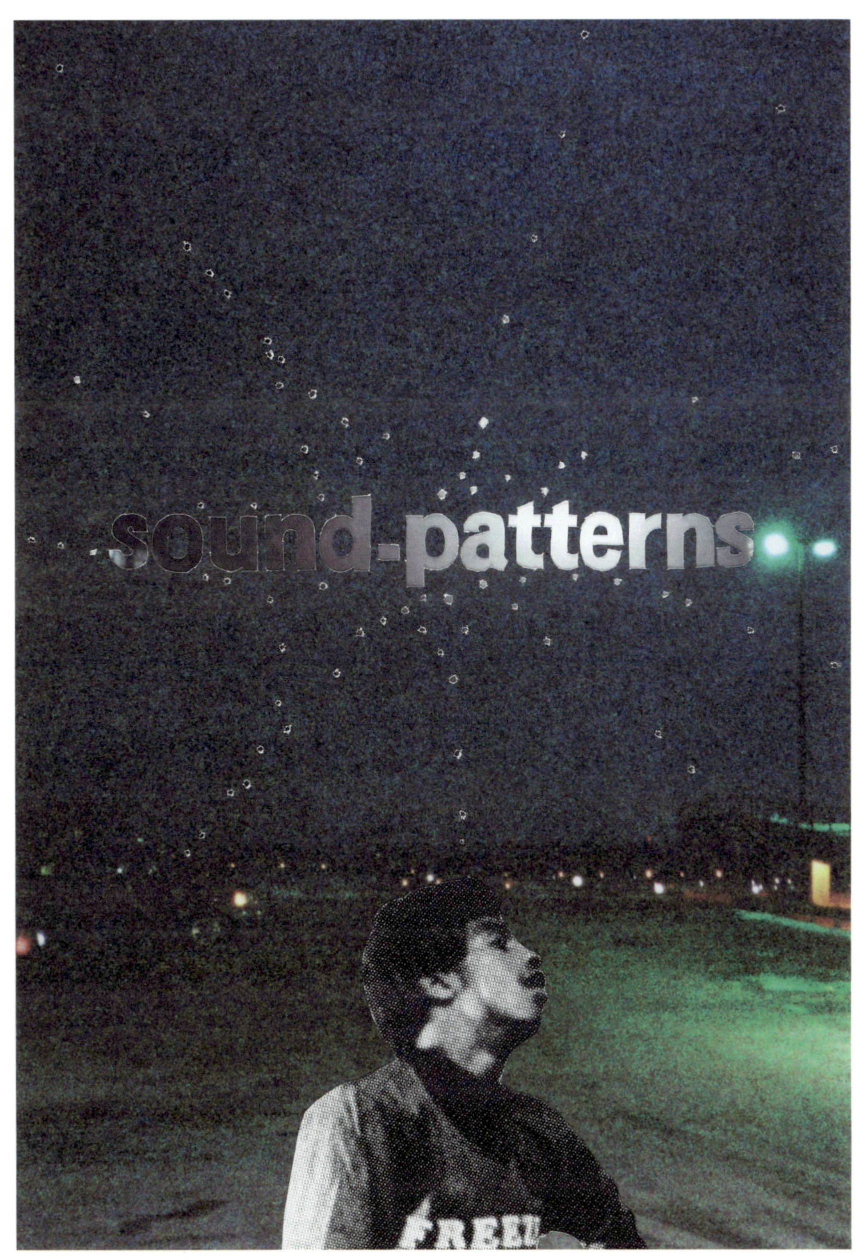
sound-patterns

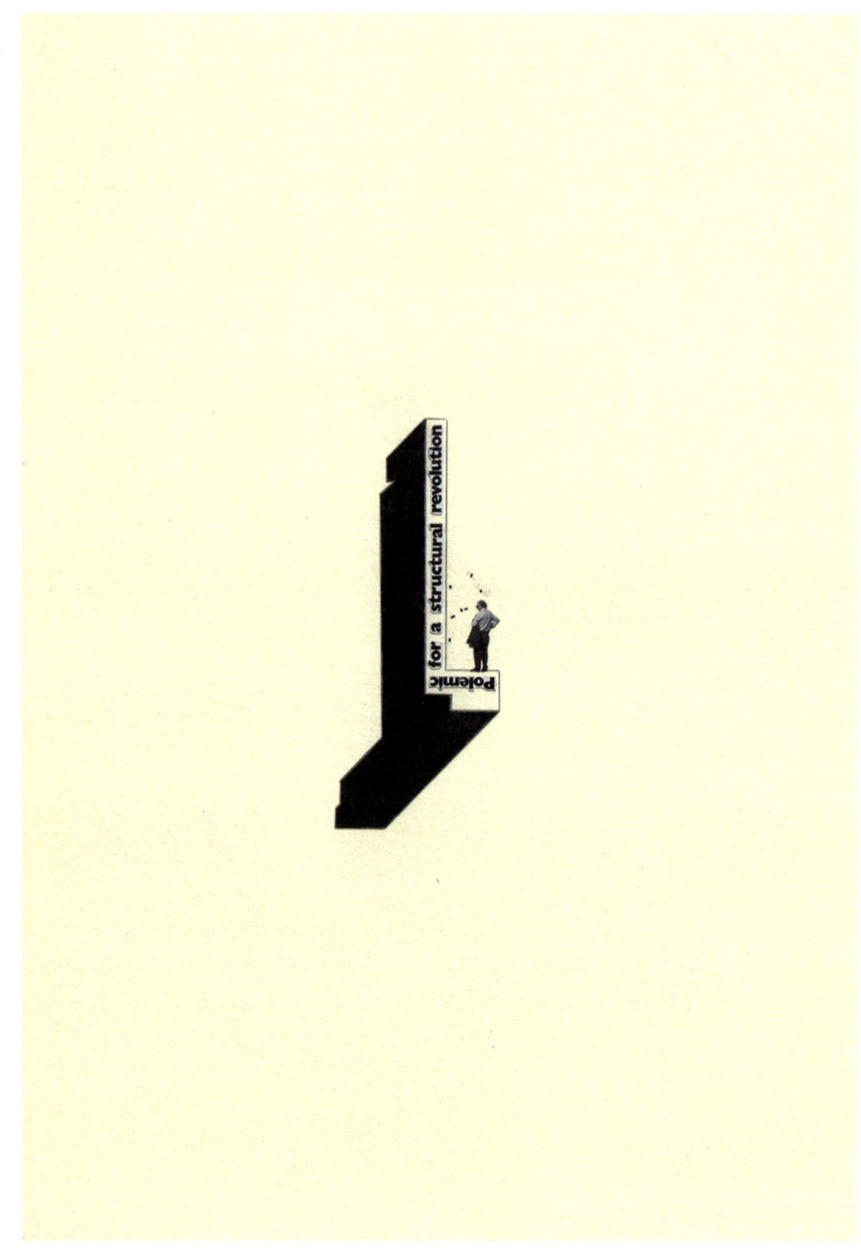

Polemic for a structural revolution

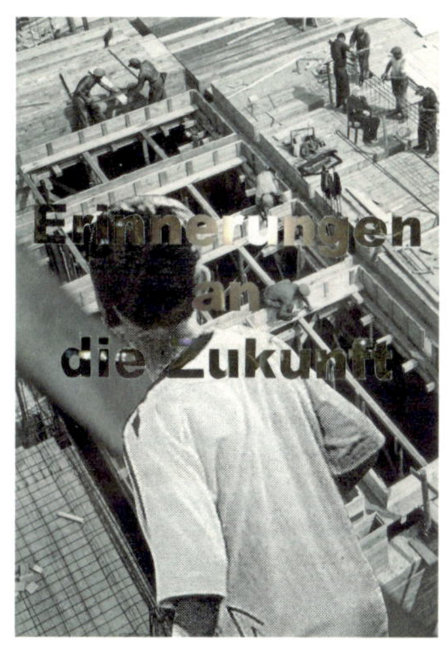
Erinnerungen
an
die Zukunft

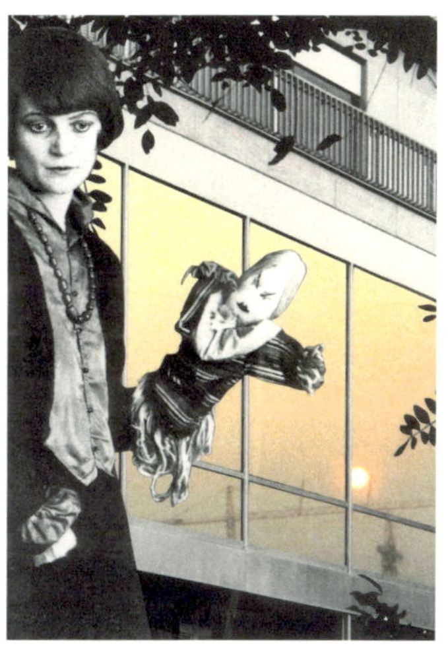

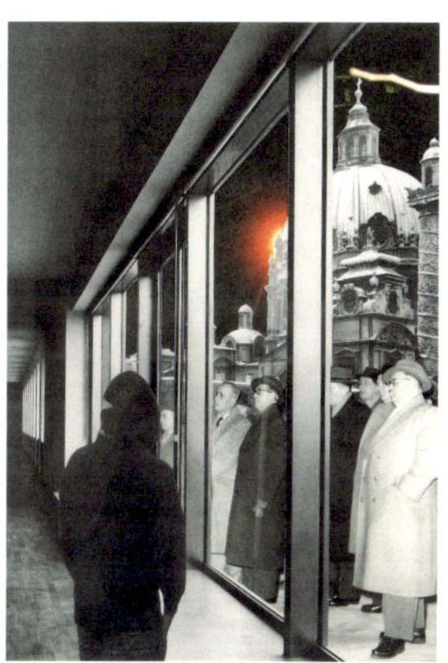

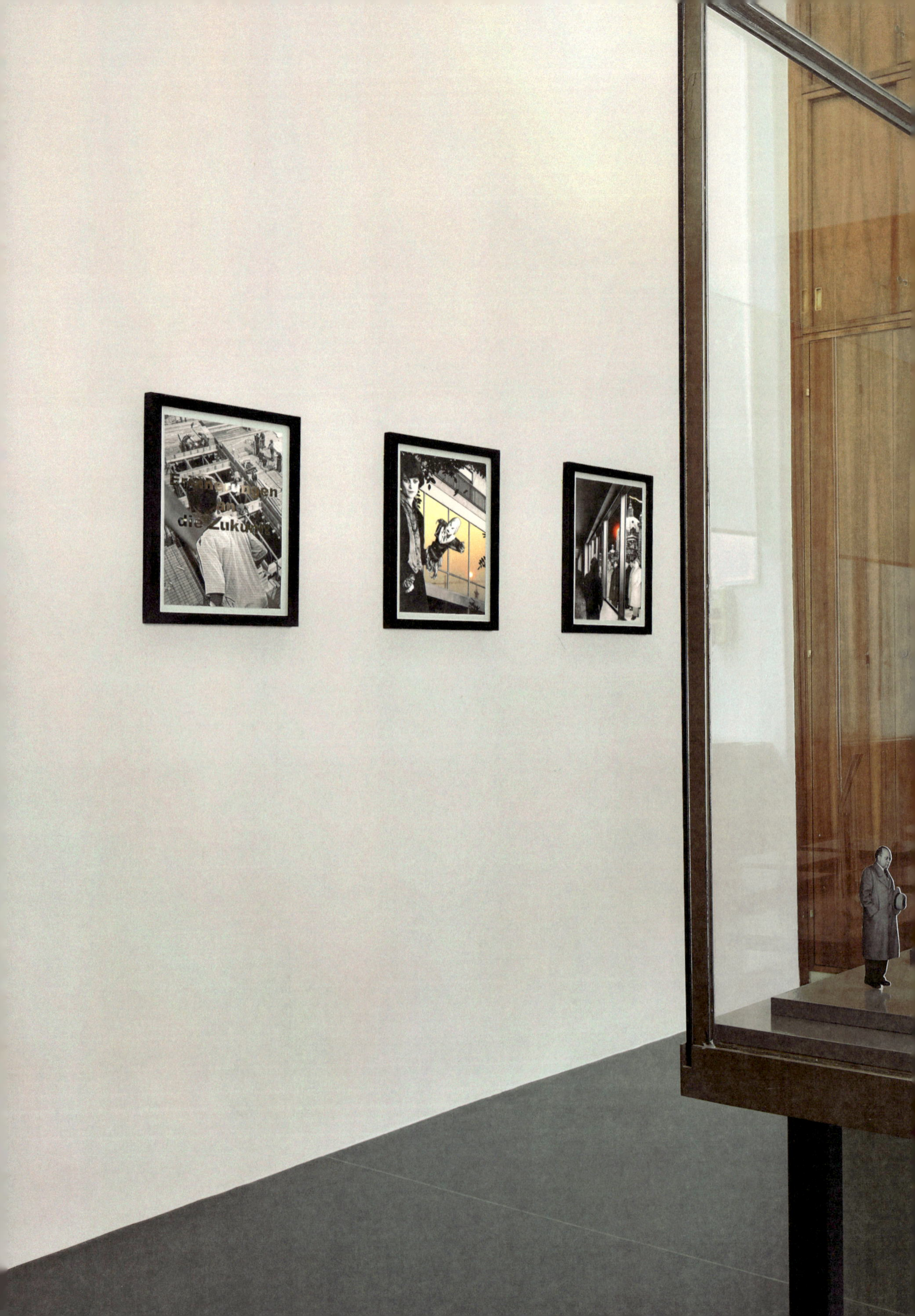

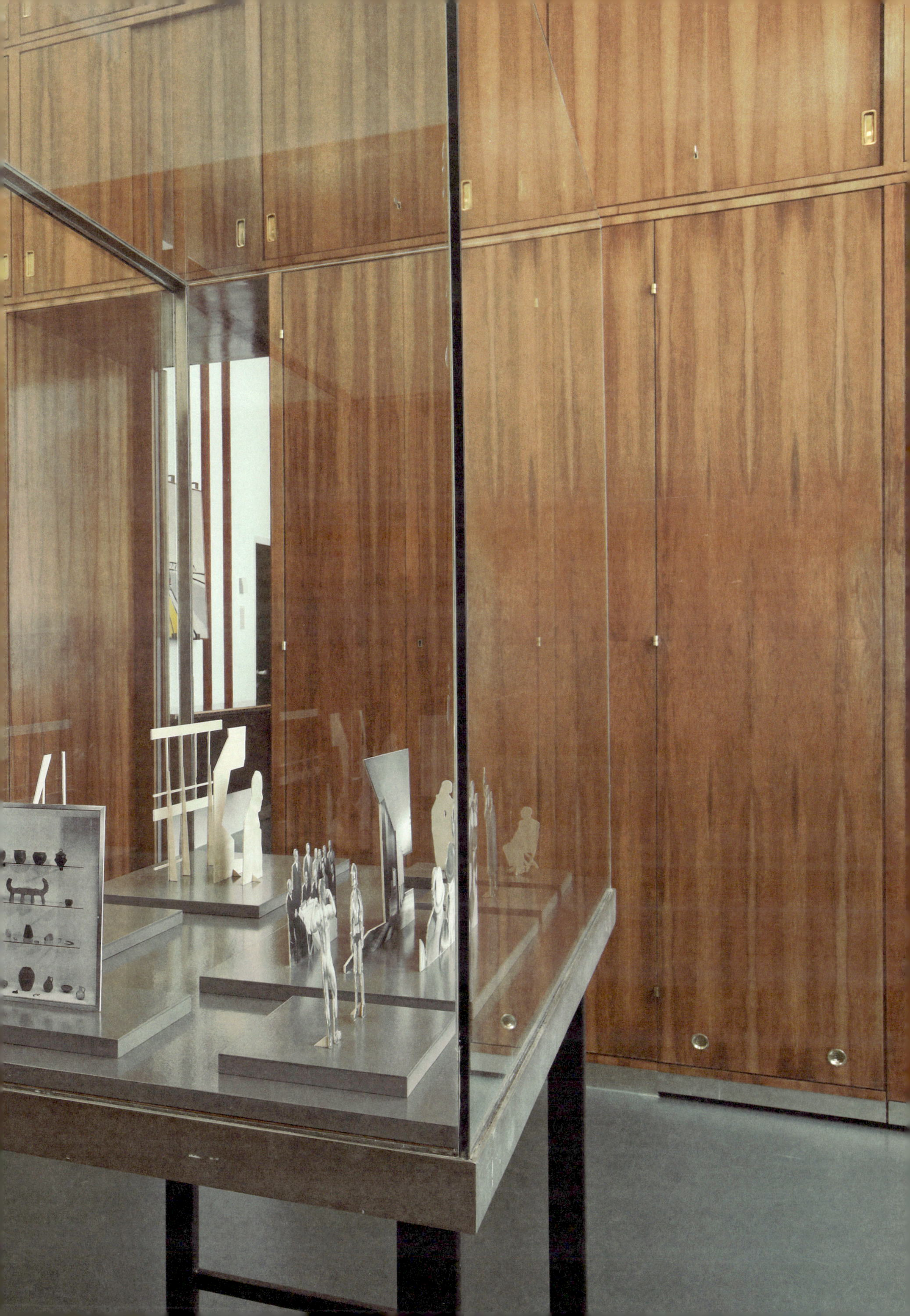

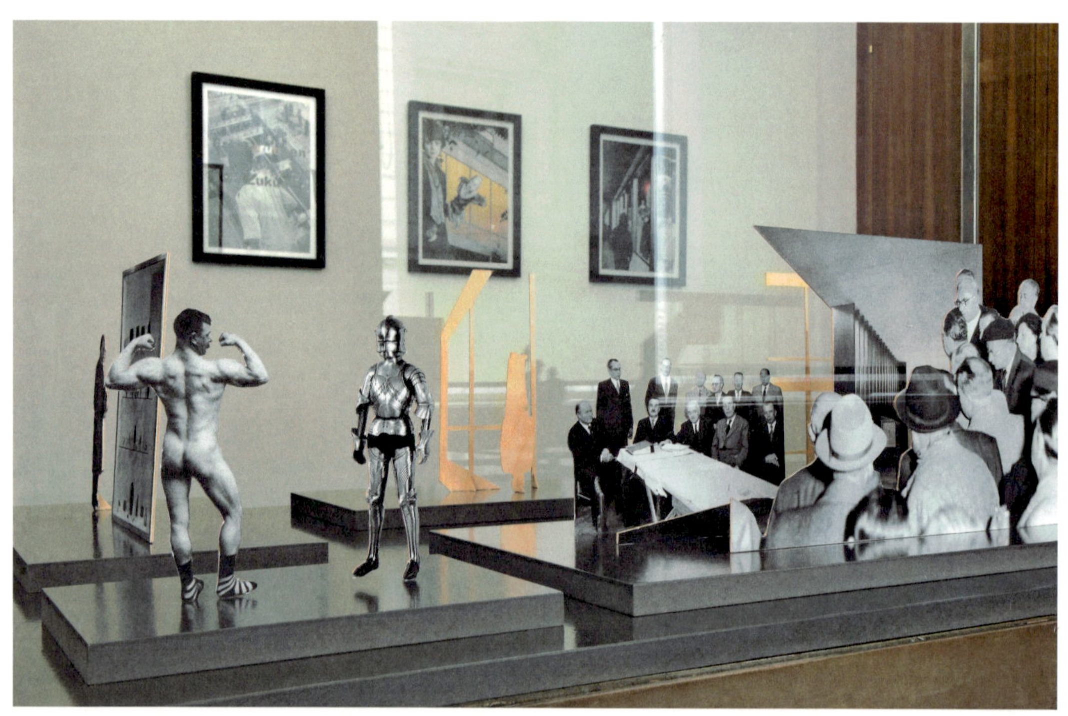

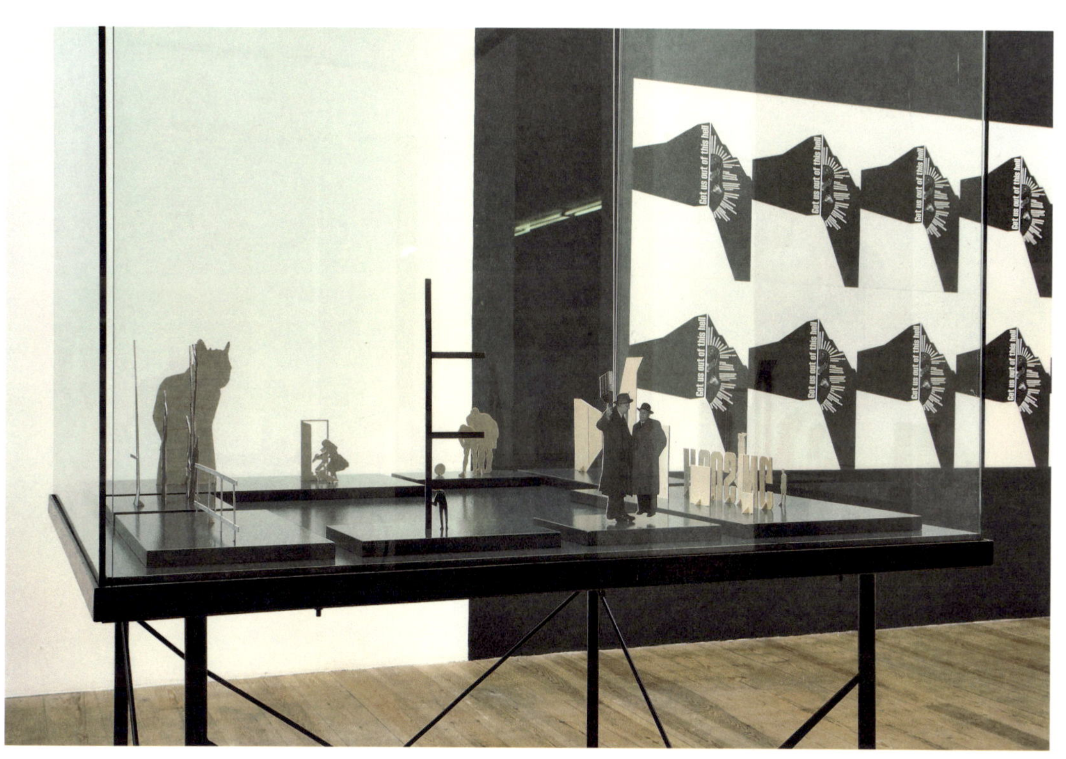

Get us out of this hell

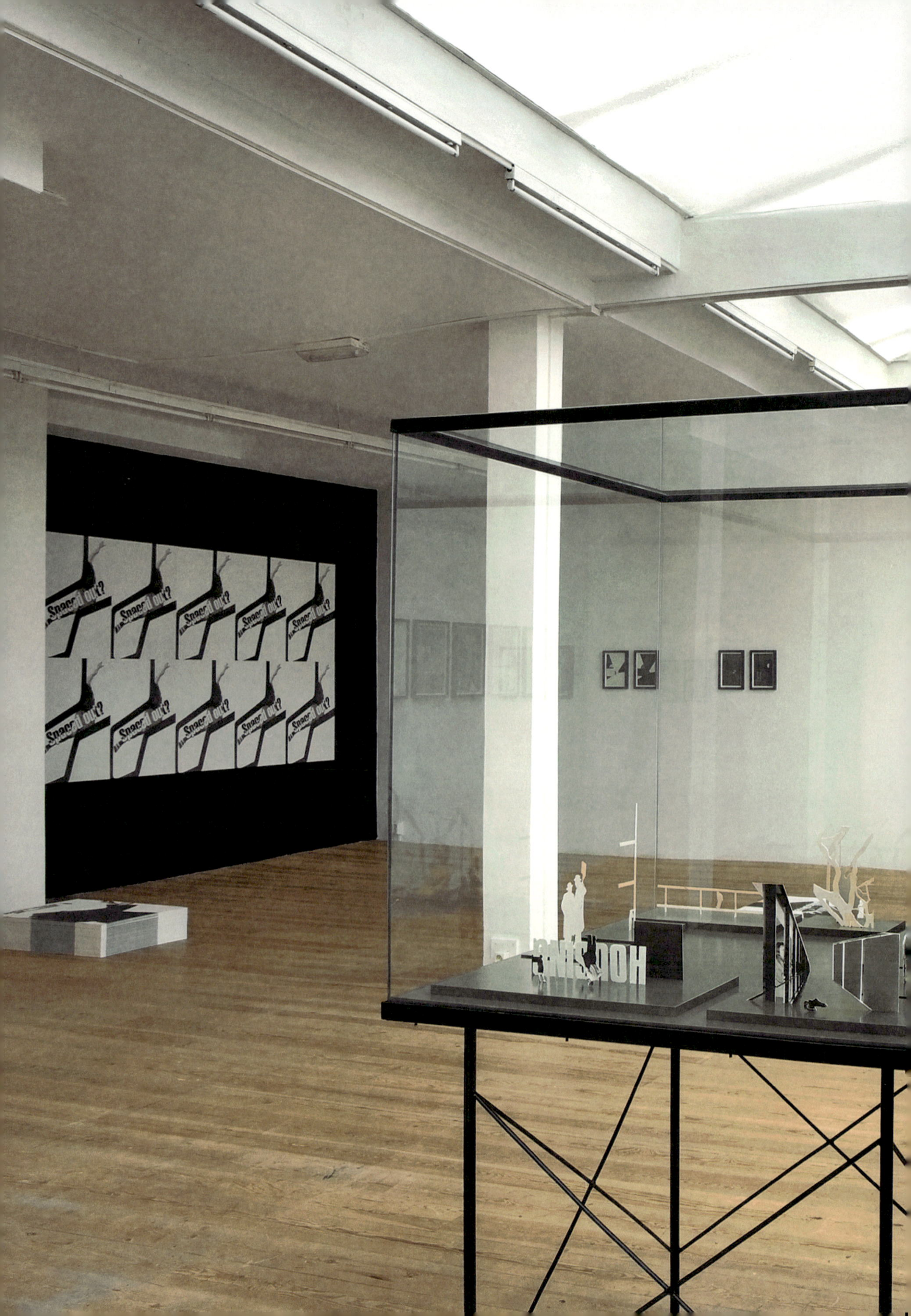
Spaced out?
HOUSING

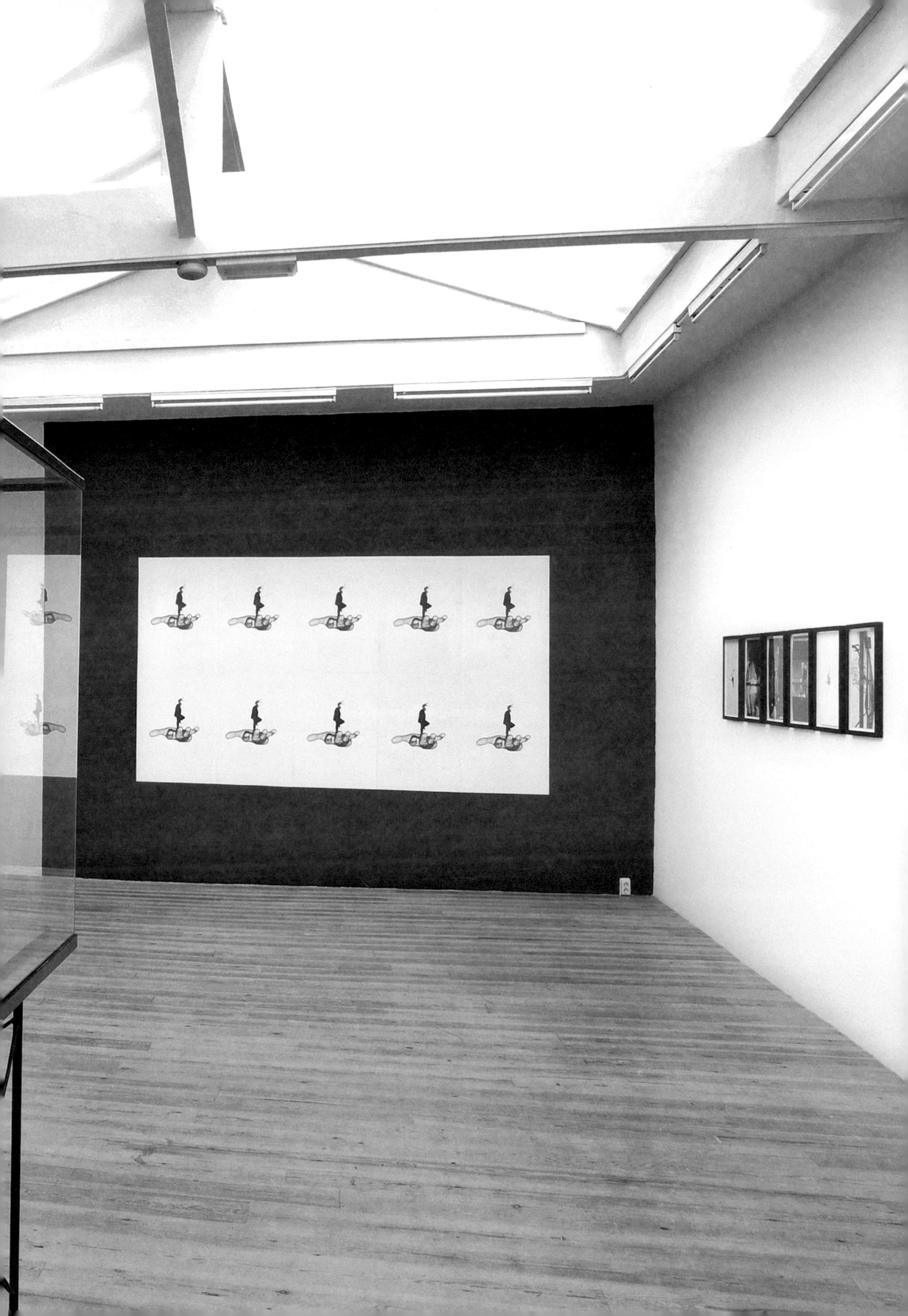

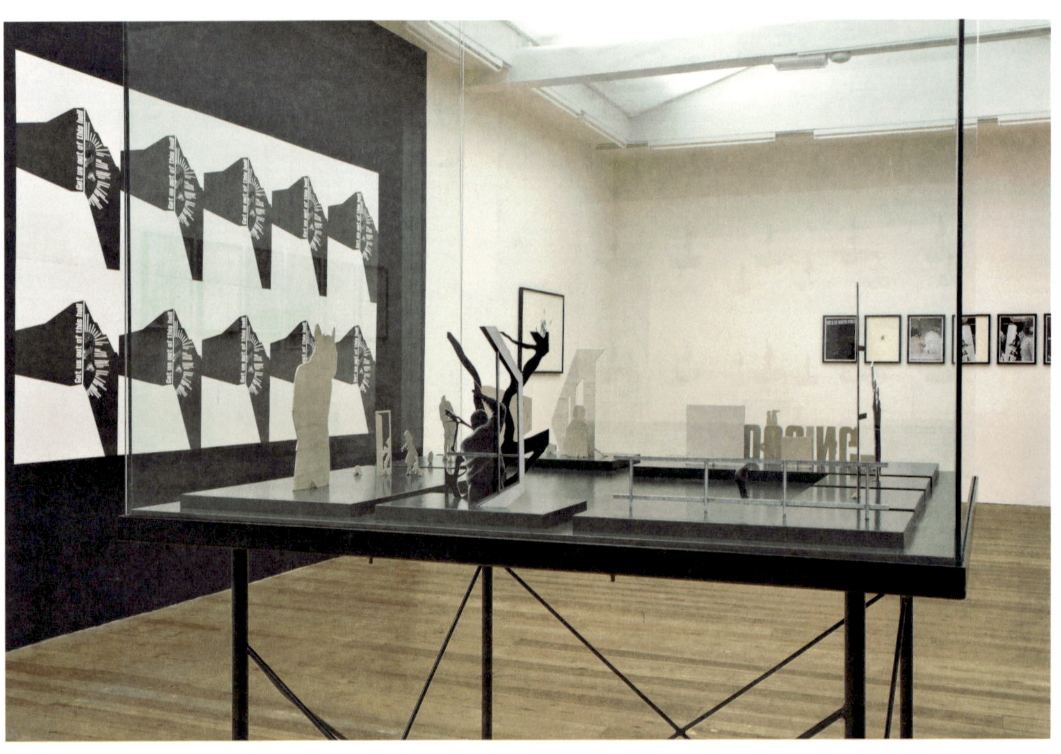

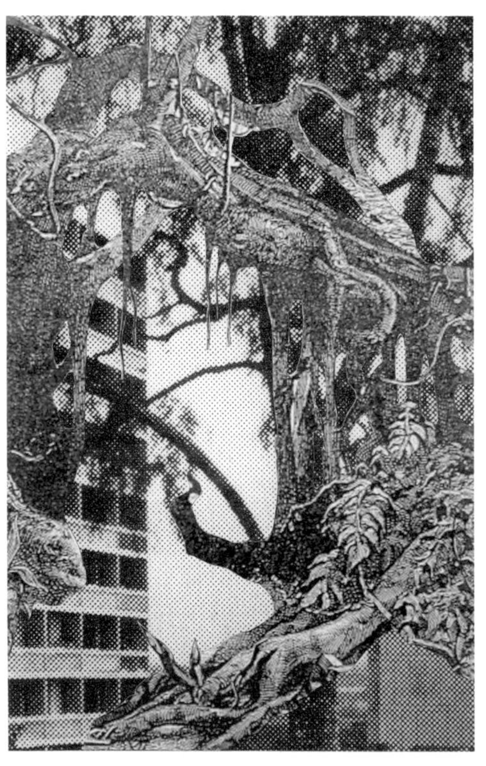 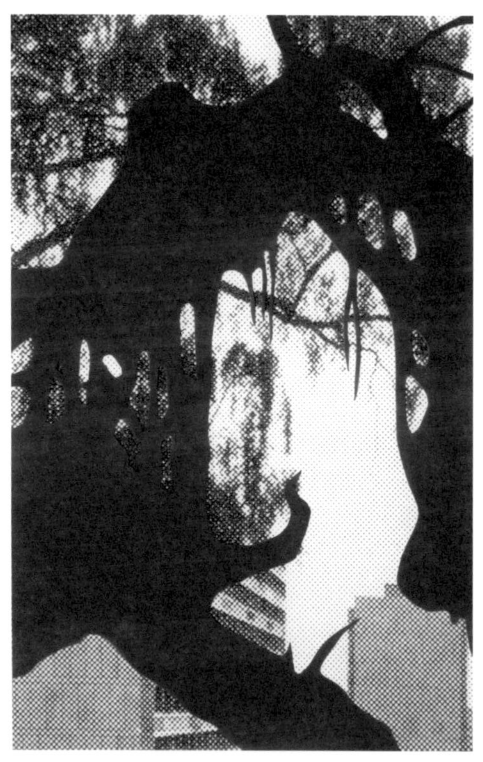

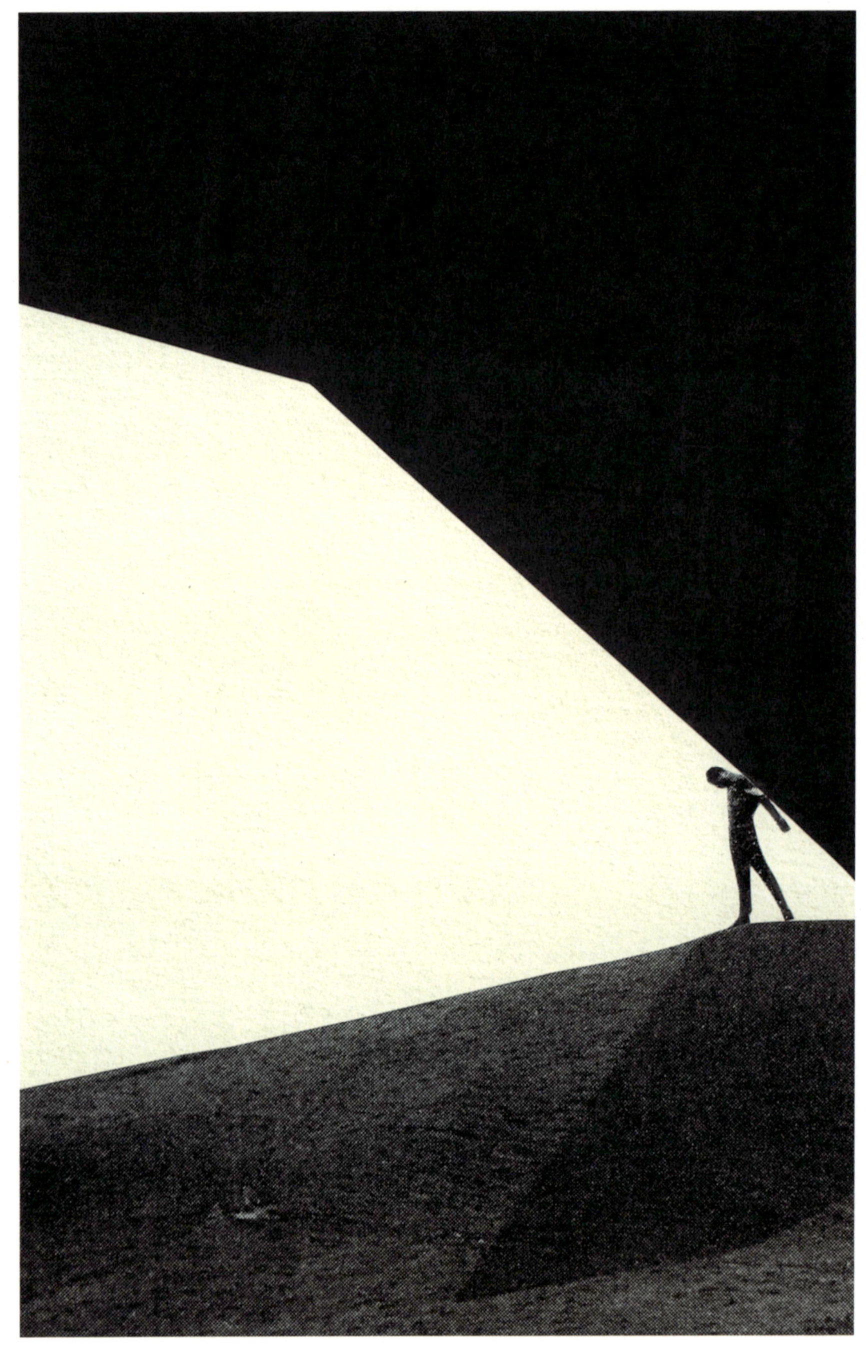

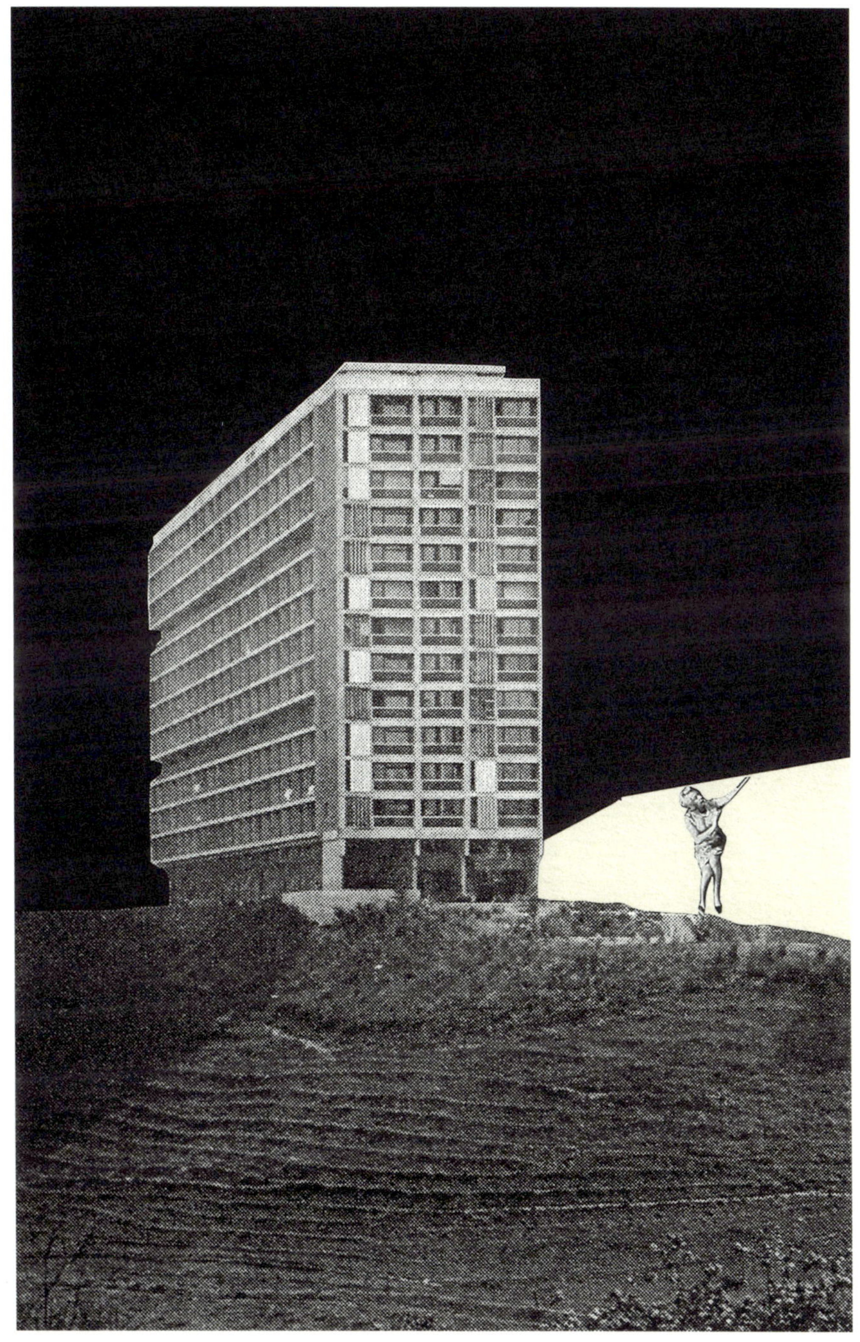

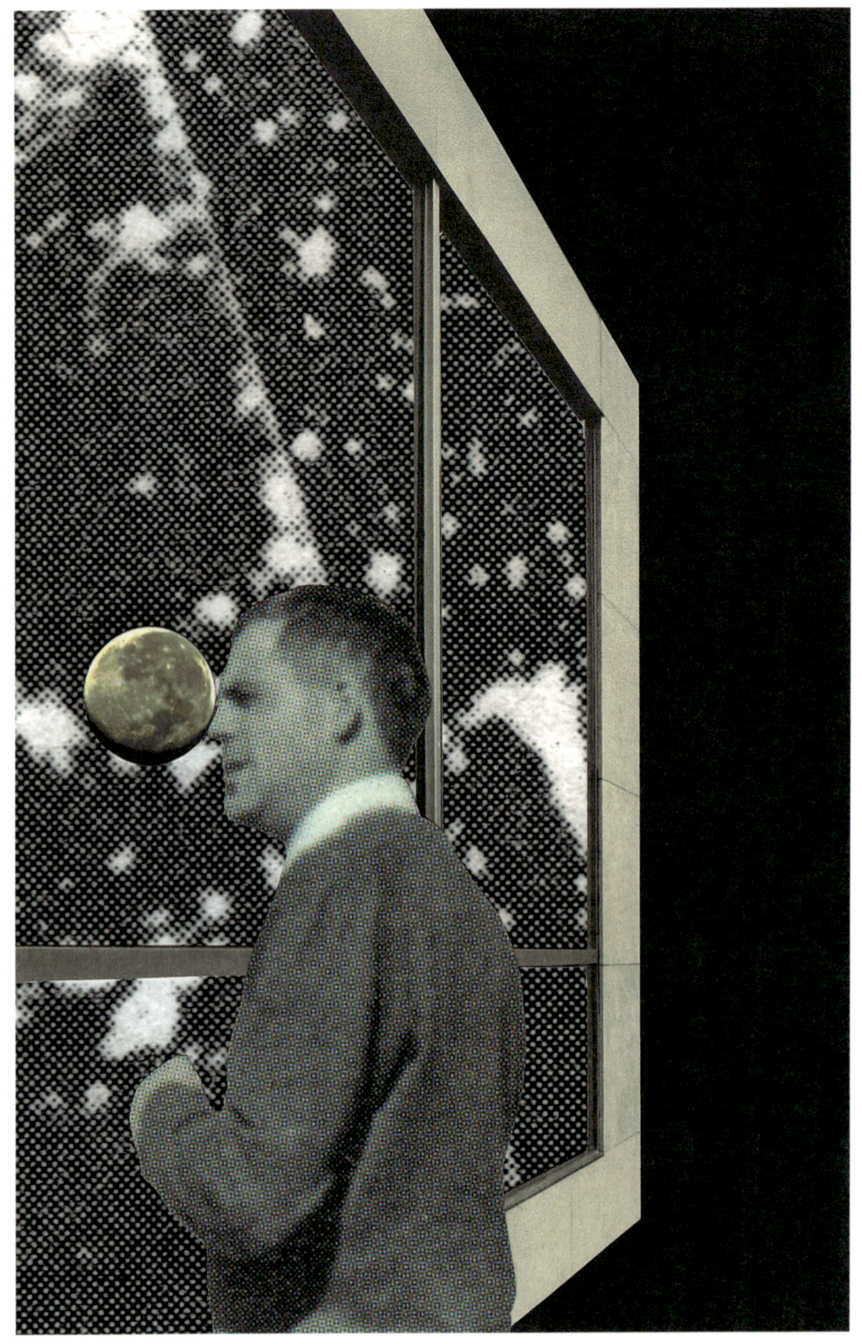

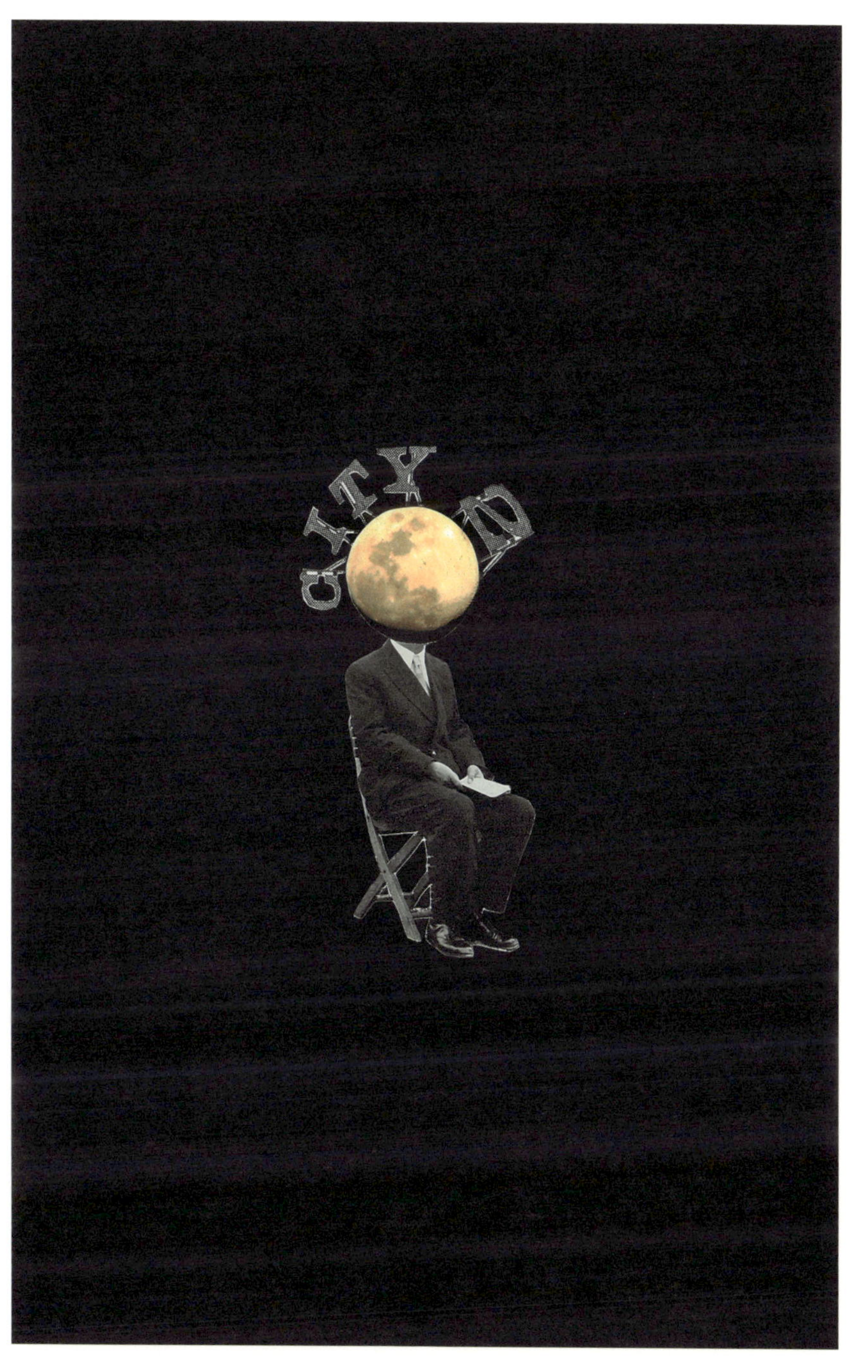
CITY
D

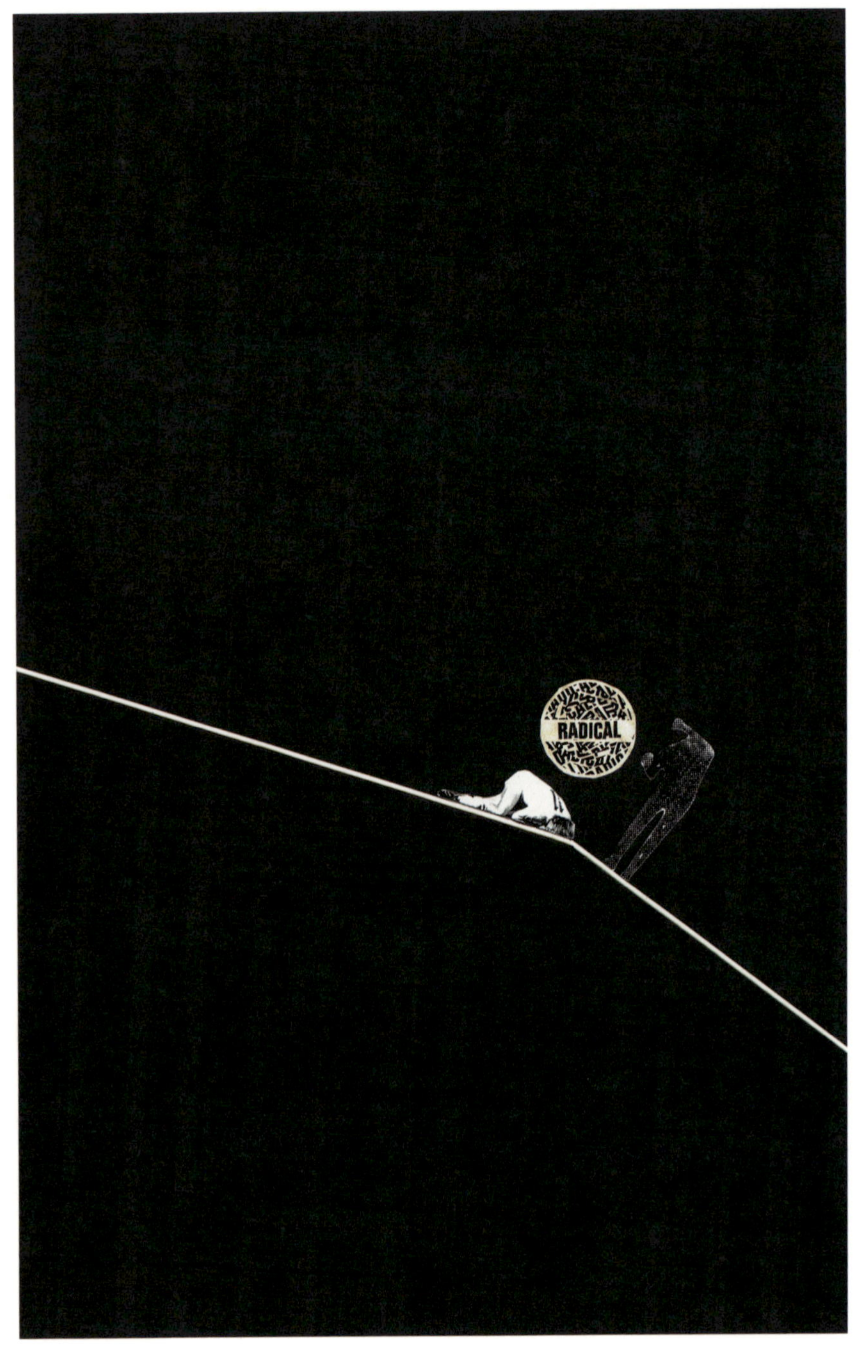
RADICAL

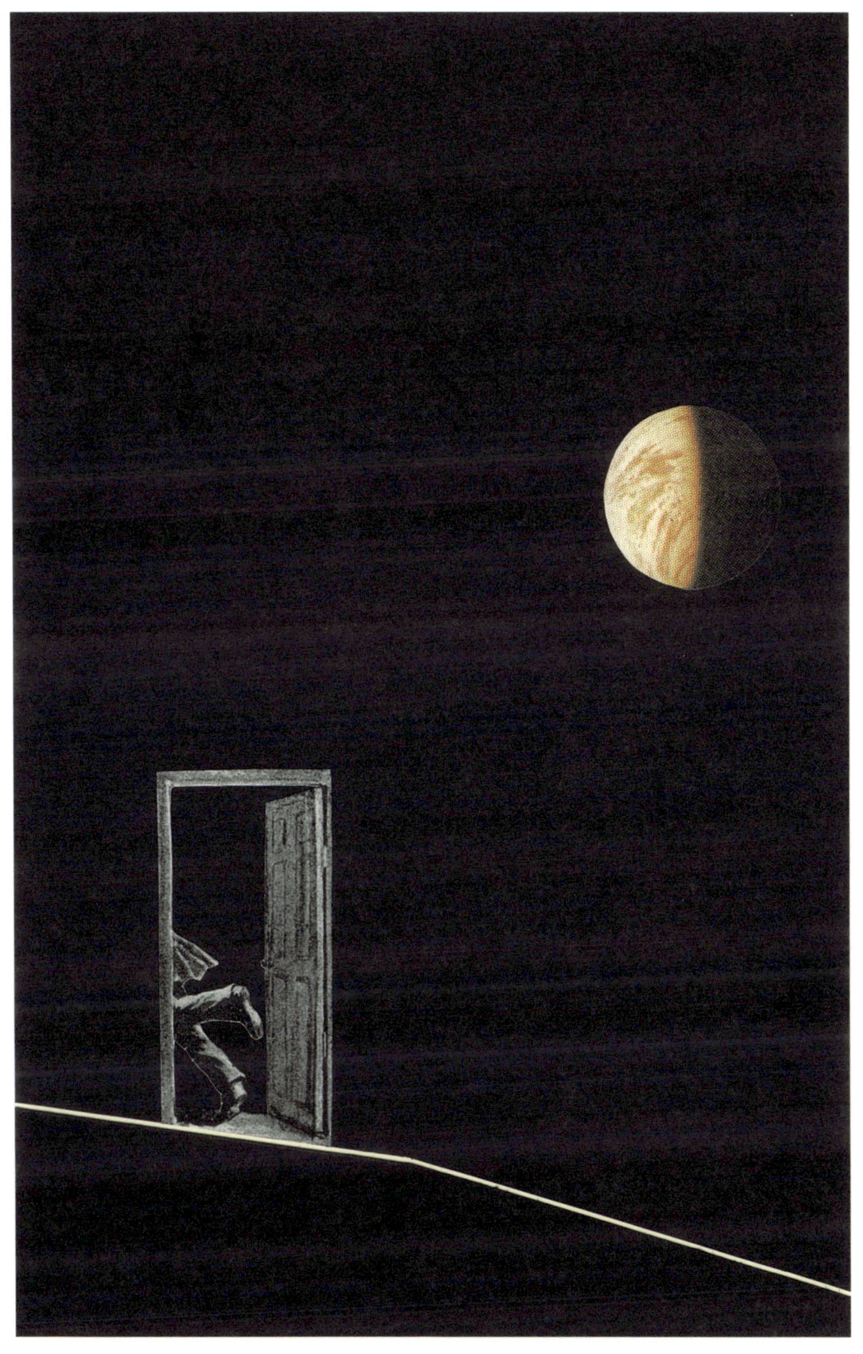

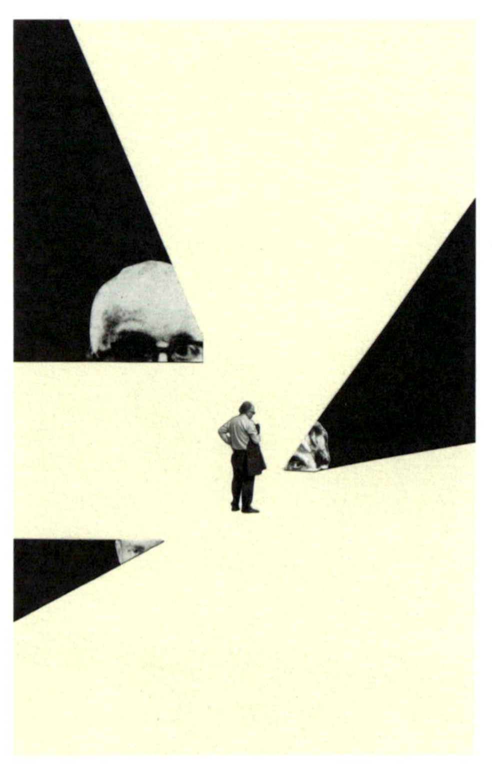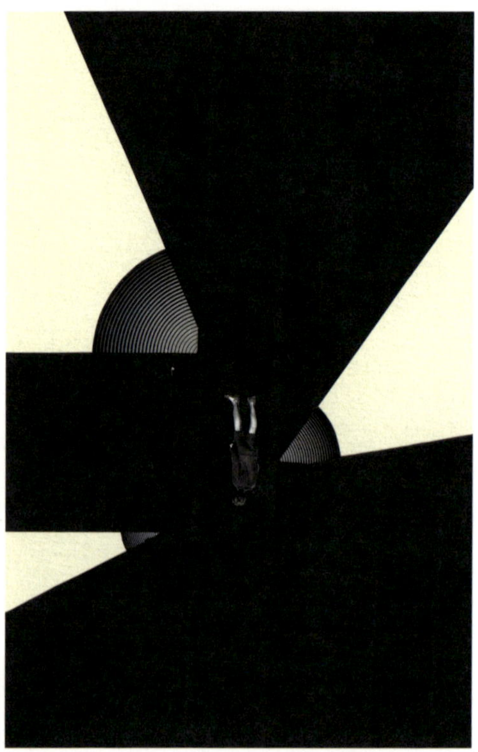

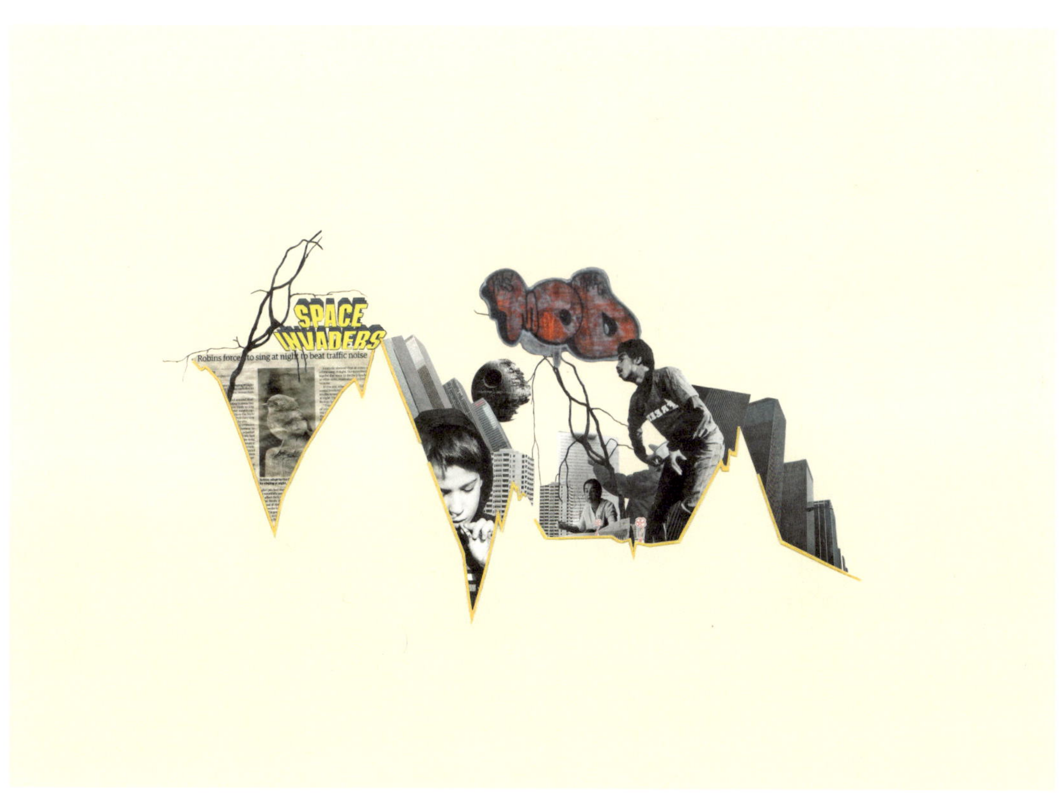

SPACE
INVADERS
Robins forced to sing at night to beat traffic noise

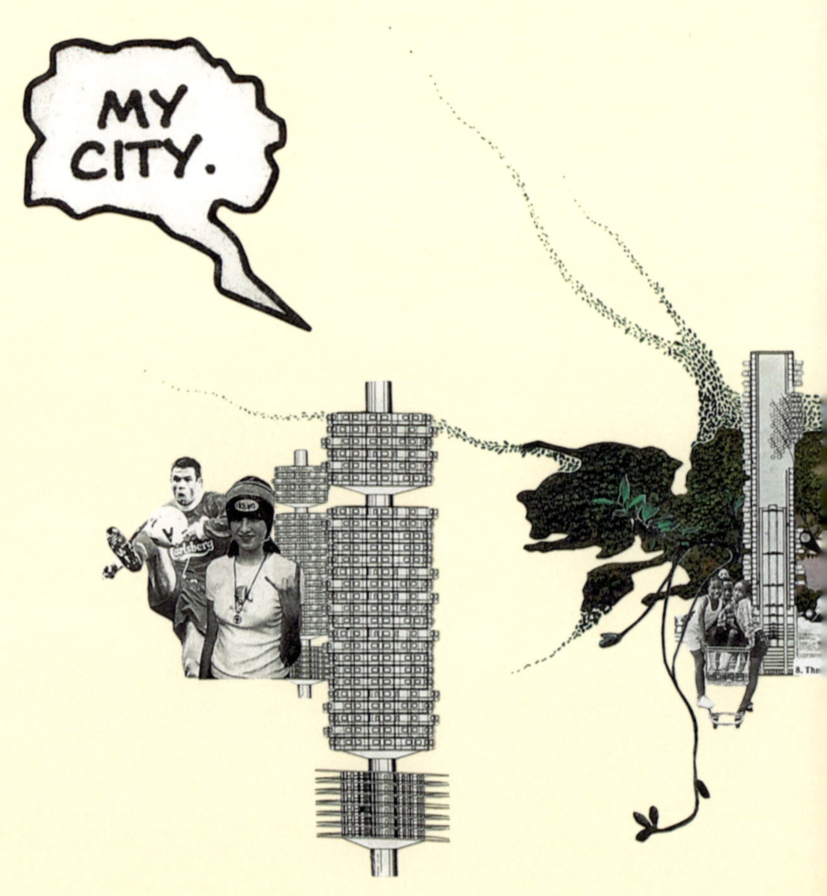
MY
CITY.

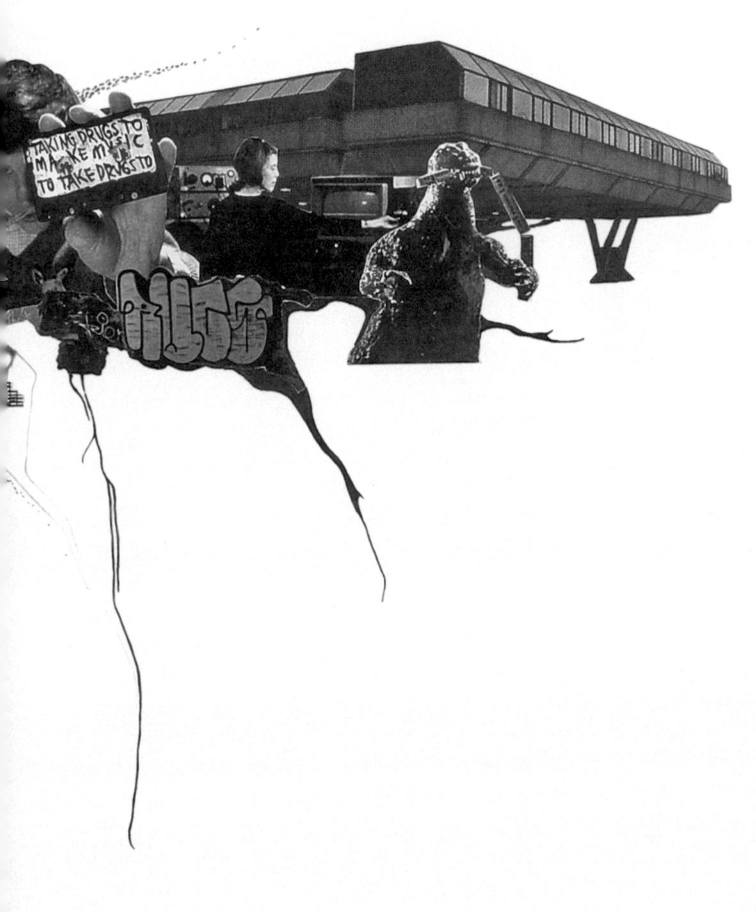
TAKING DRUGS TO
MAKE MUSIC
TO TAKE DRUGS TO

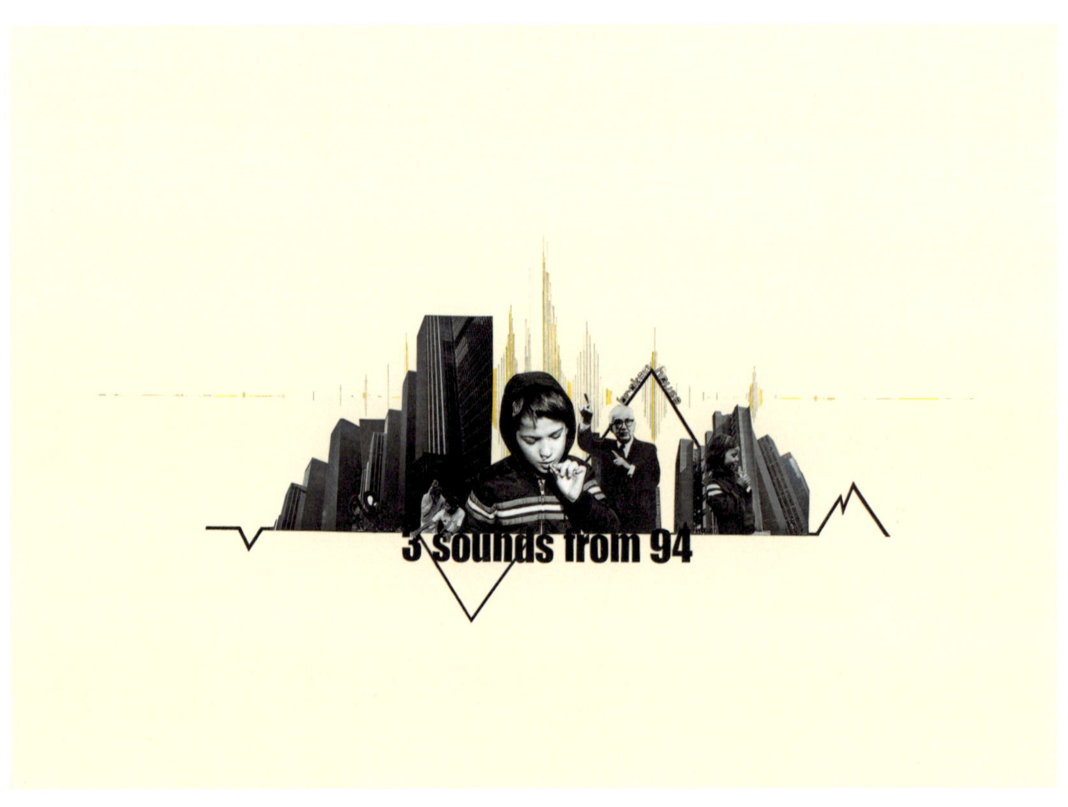

5 sounds from 94

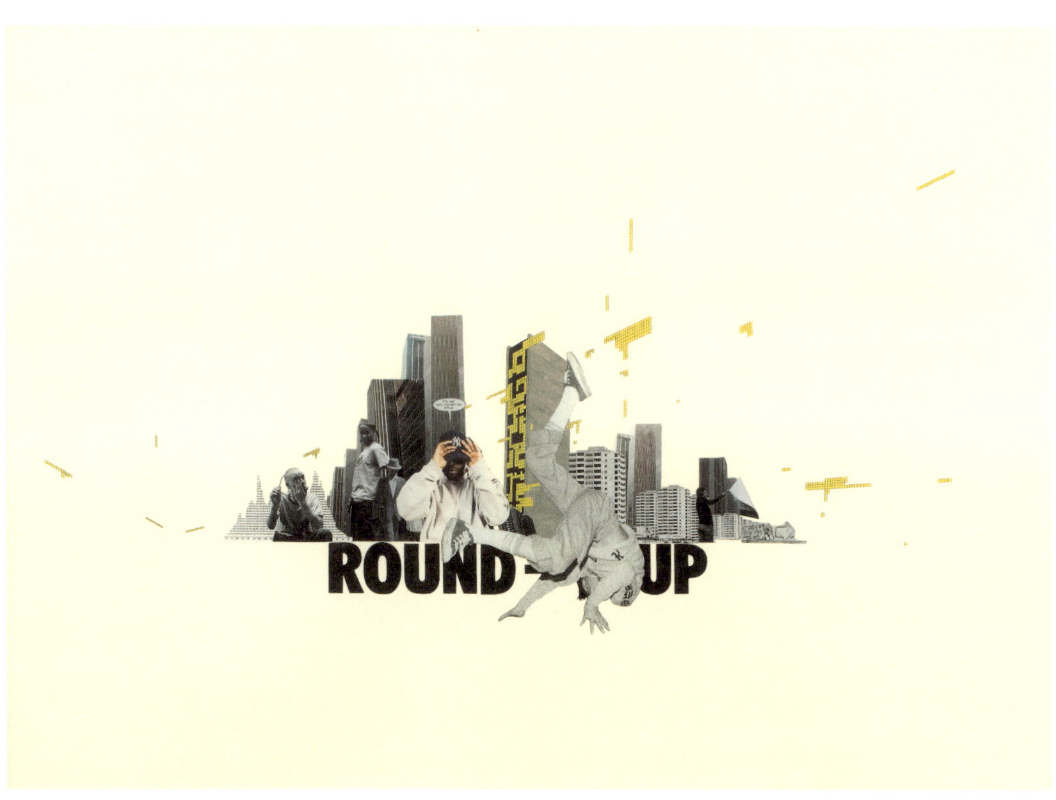
ROUND-UP

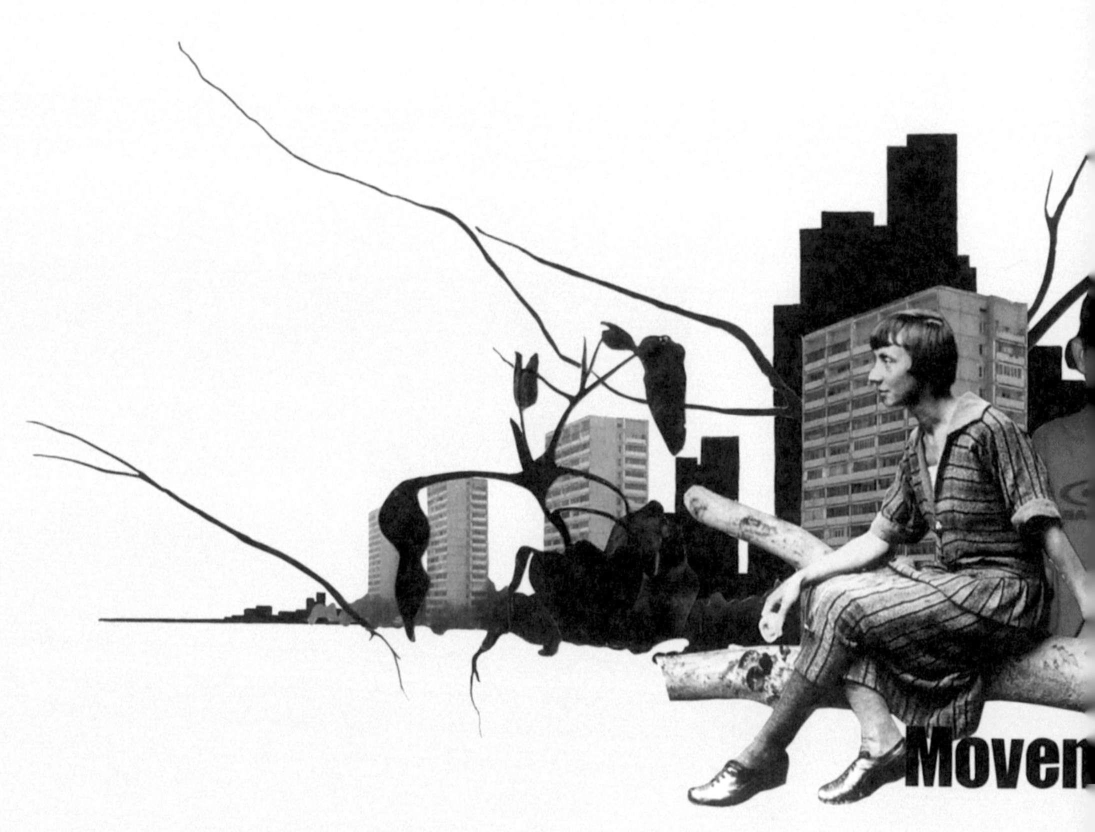
Movem

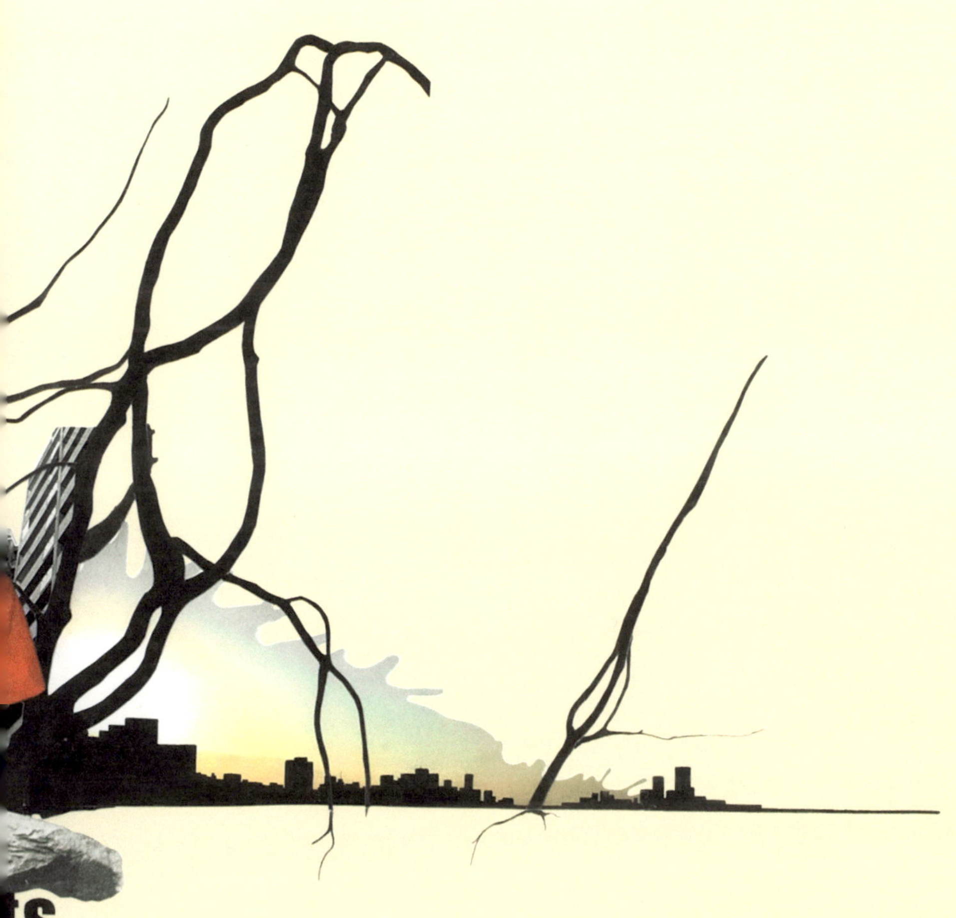

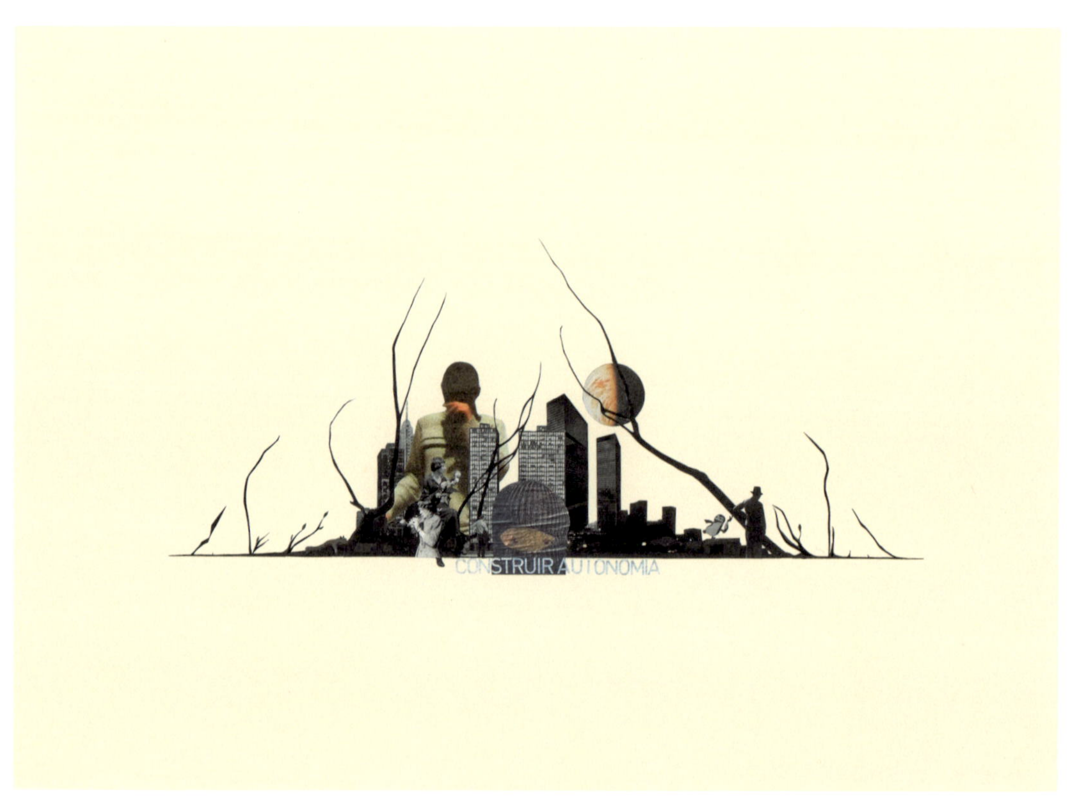

CONSTRUIR AUTONOMÍA

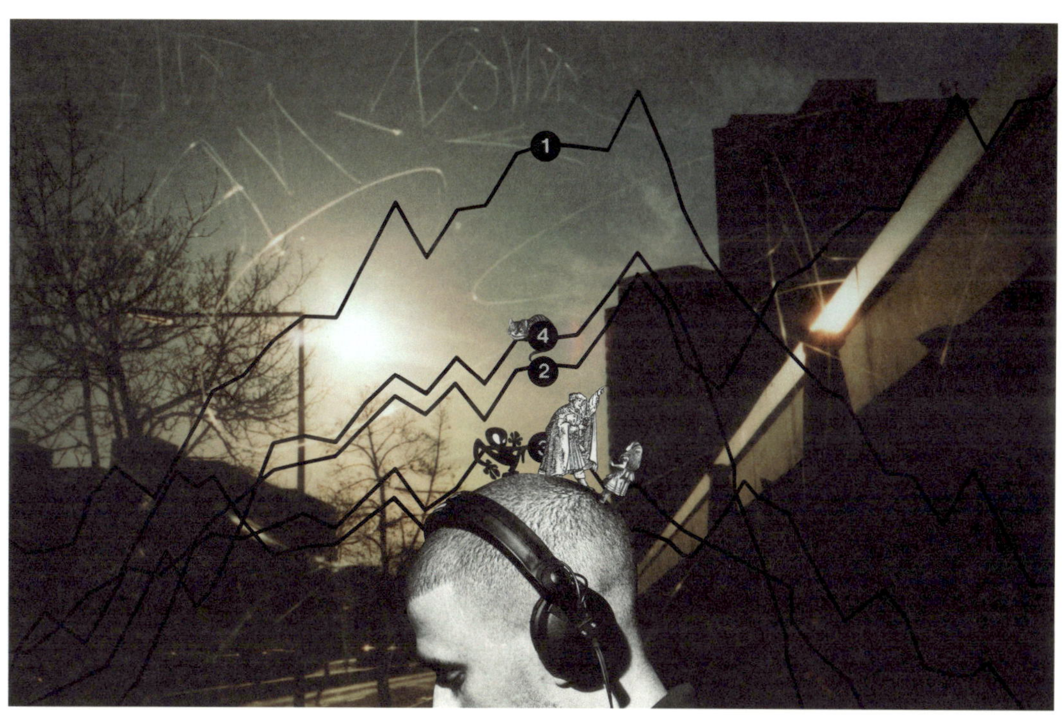

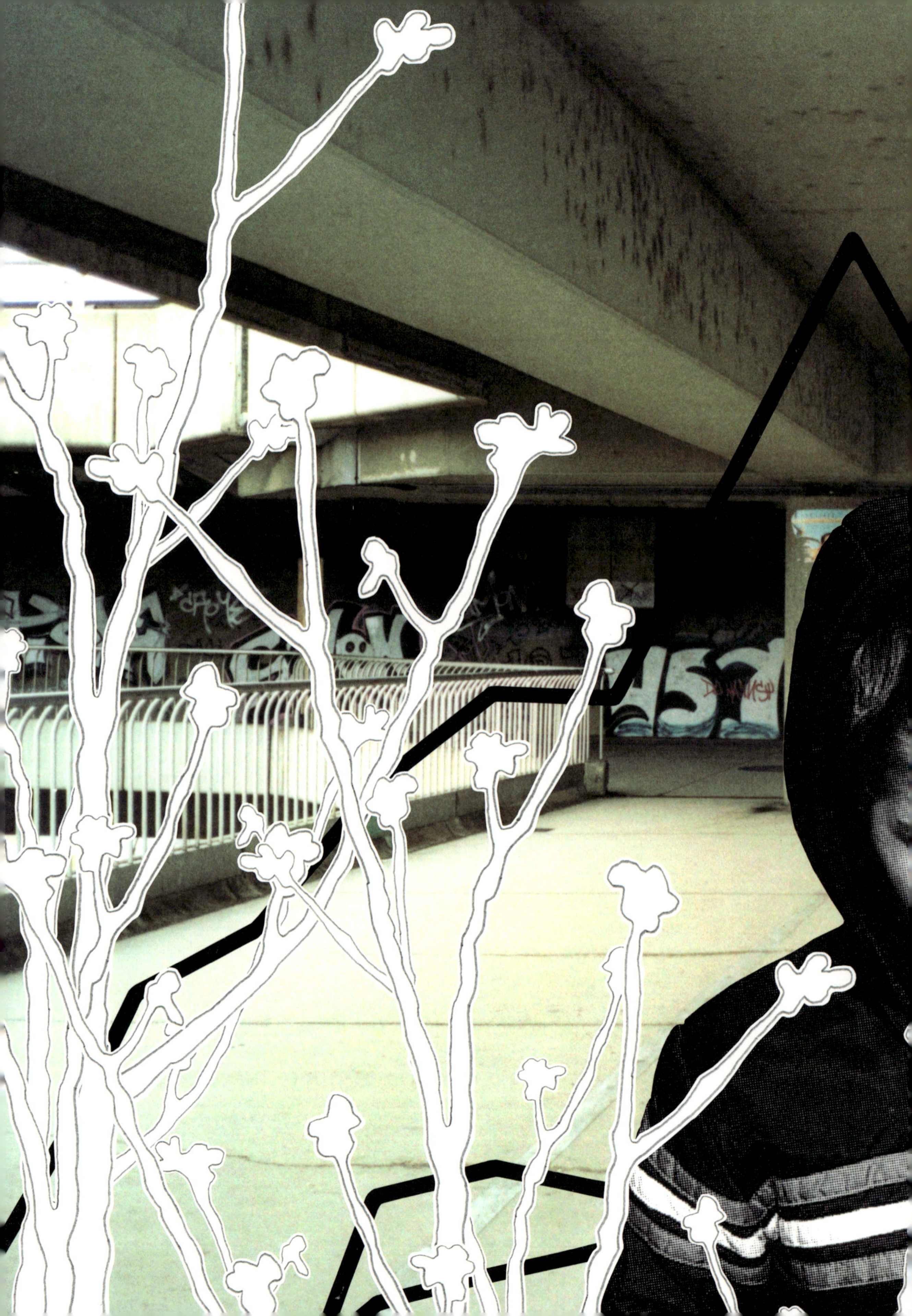

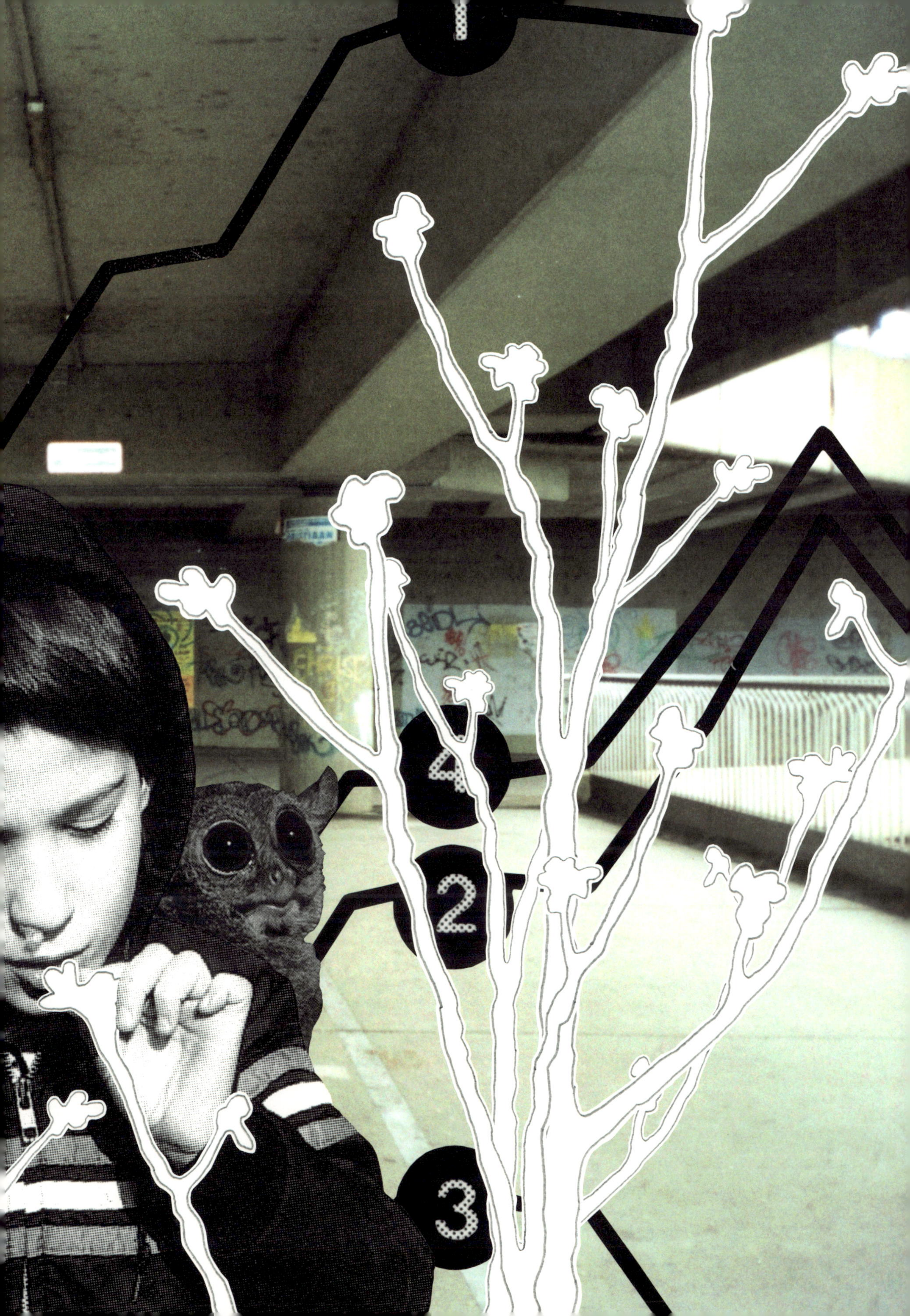

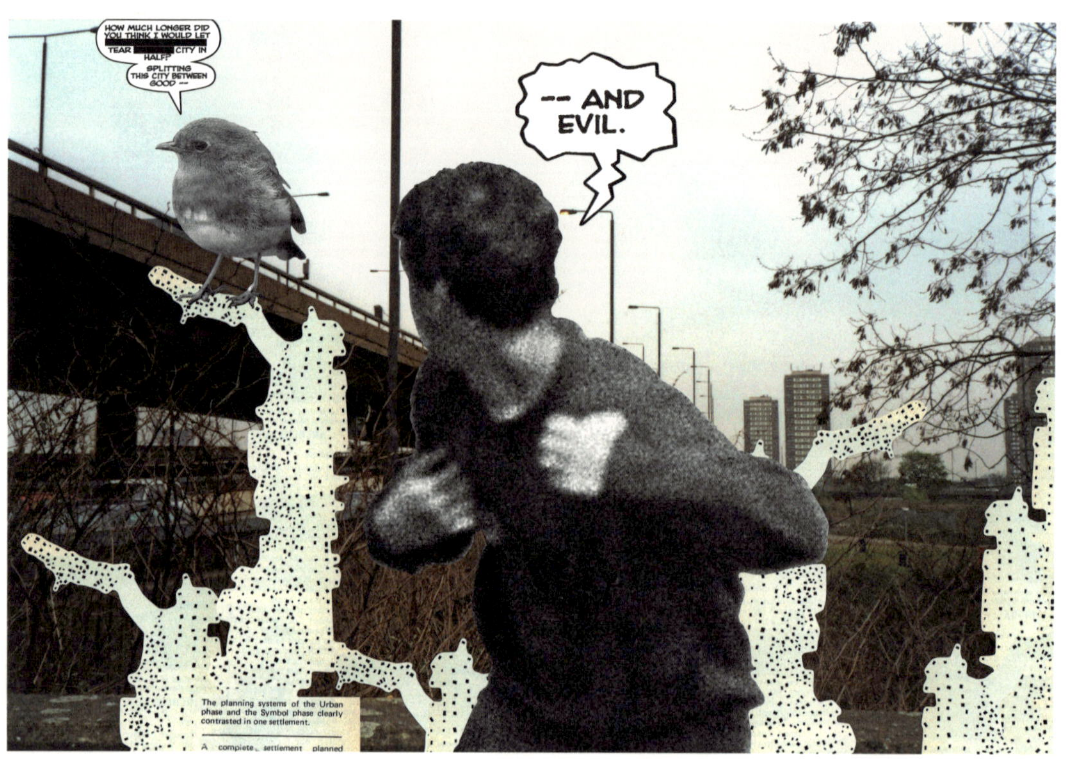

HOW MUCH LONGER DID YOU THINK I WOULD LET ██████ TEAR ████ CITY IN HALF?
SPLITTING THIS CITY BETWEEN GOOD --
-- AND EVIL.
The planning systems of the Urban phase and the Symbol phase clearly contrasted in one settlement.
A complete, settlement planned

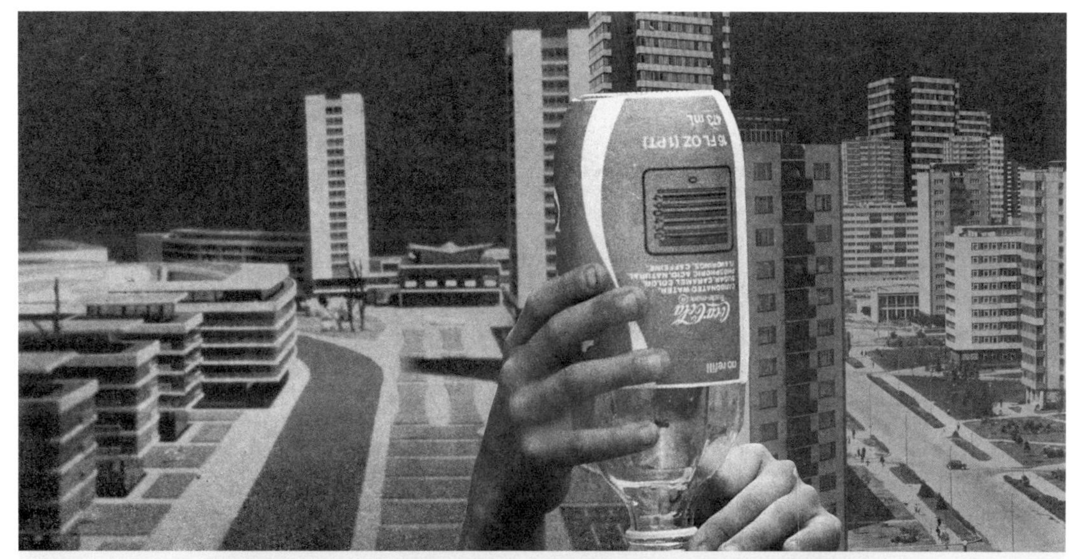

Urbano planiranje i lokalne inicijative

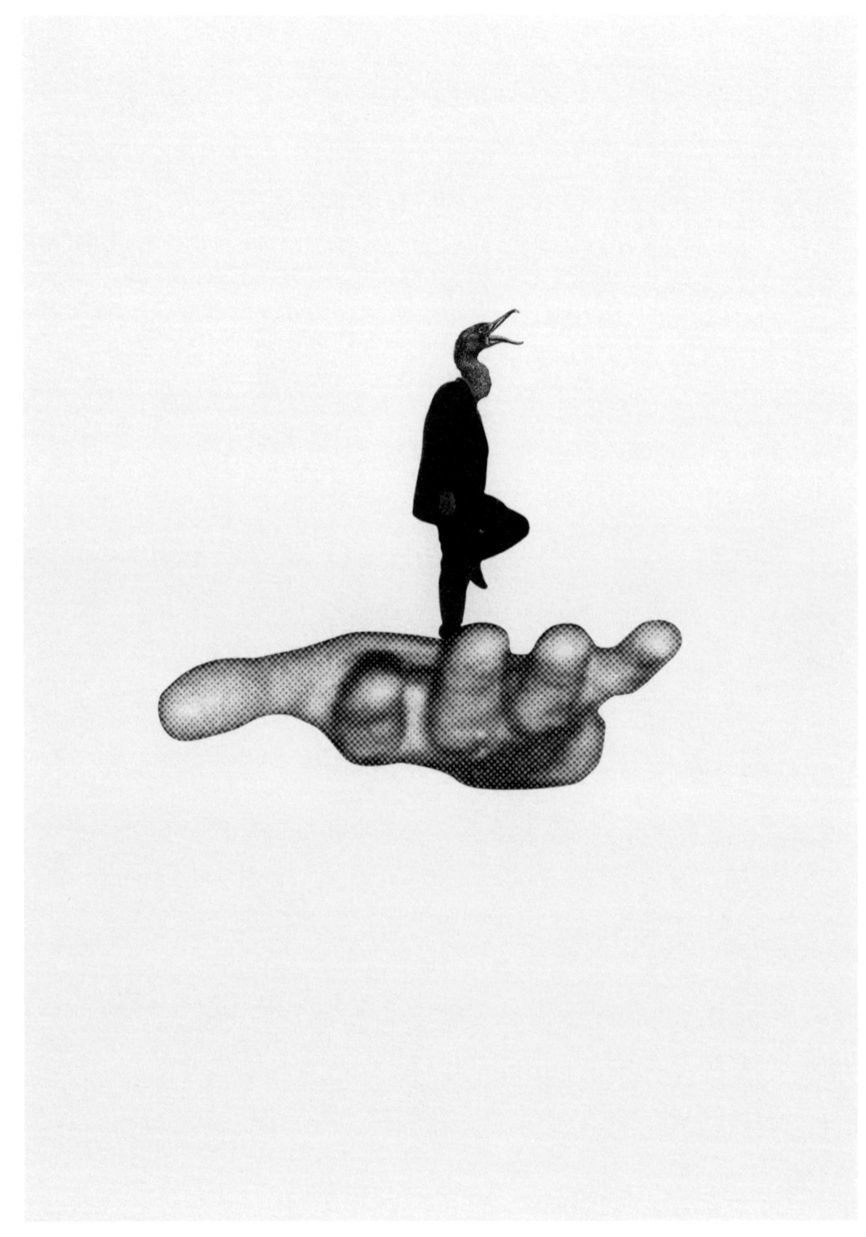

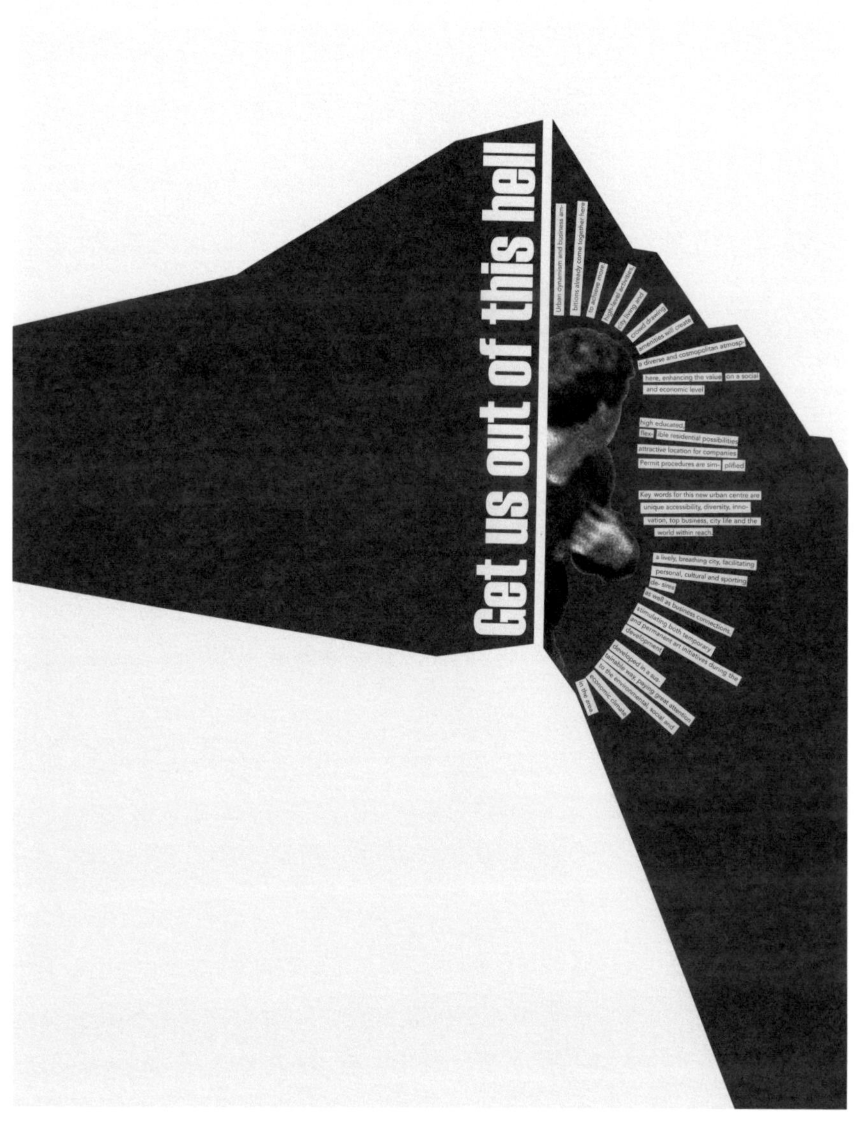

Get us out of this hell
Urban dynamism and business am-
bitions already come together here
To achieve more
high-level architects will create
a diverse and cosmopolitan atmosp-
here, enhancing the value on a social
and economic level
high educated.
flexible residential possibilities
attractive location for companies
Permit procedures are sim- plified
Key words for this new urban centre are
unique accessibility, diversity, inno-
vation, top business, city life and the
world within reach.
a lively, breathing city, facilitating
personal, cultural and sporting
de- sires
as well as business connections
and permanent art interests during the
development
Developed in a dus...

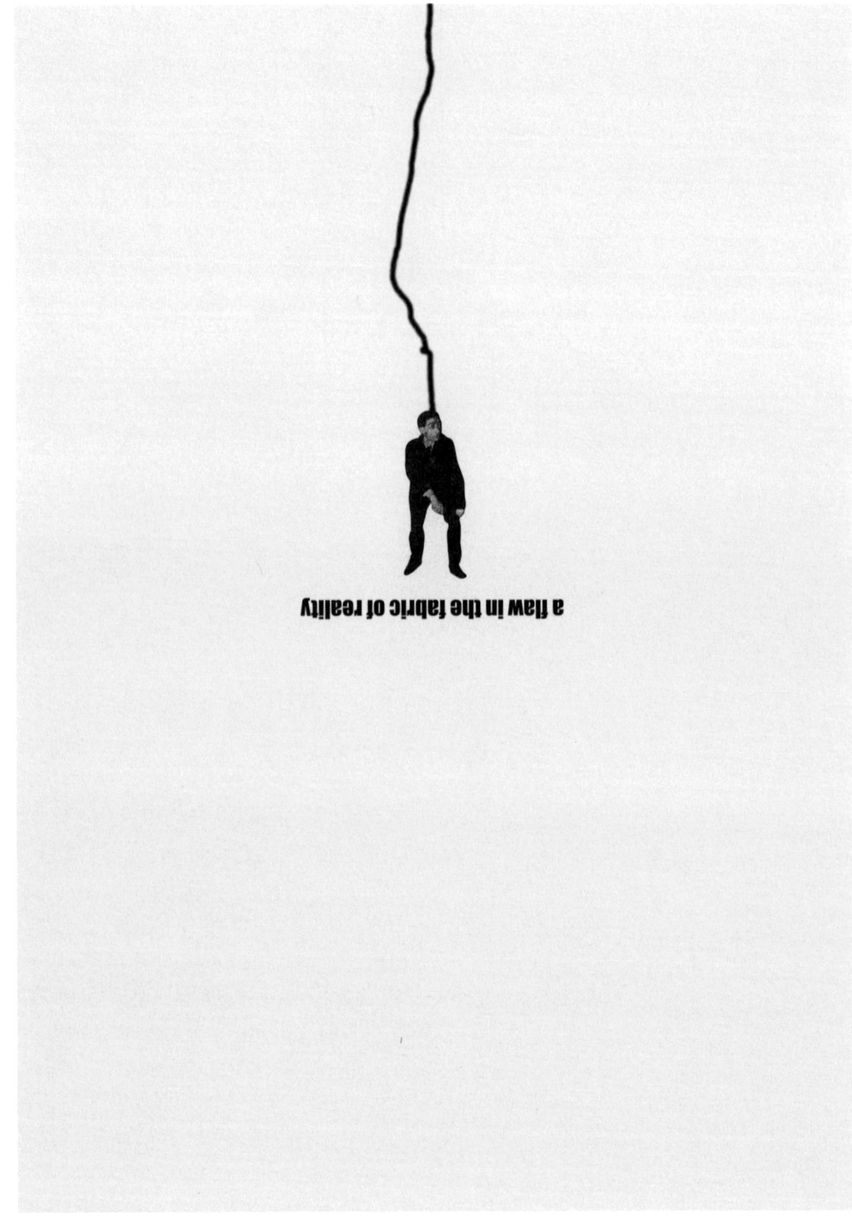
a flaw in the fabric of reality

Spatial Domination and Resistance

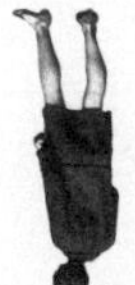

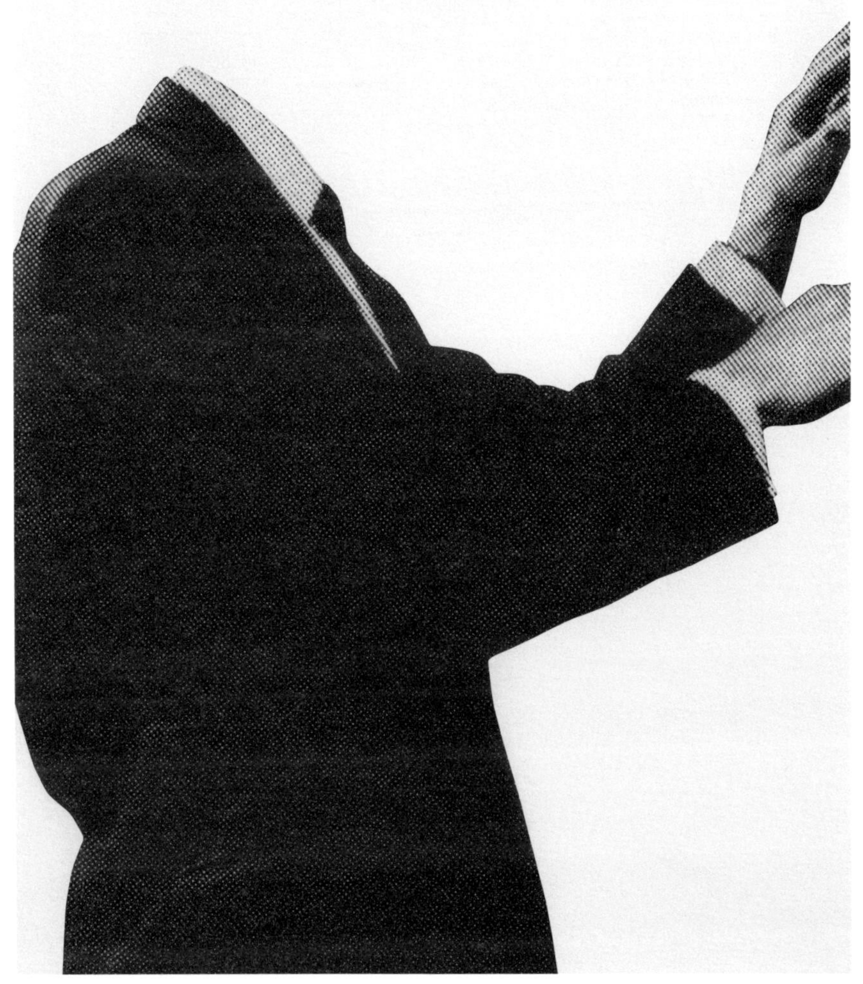

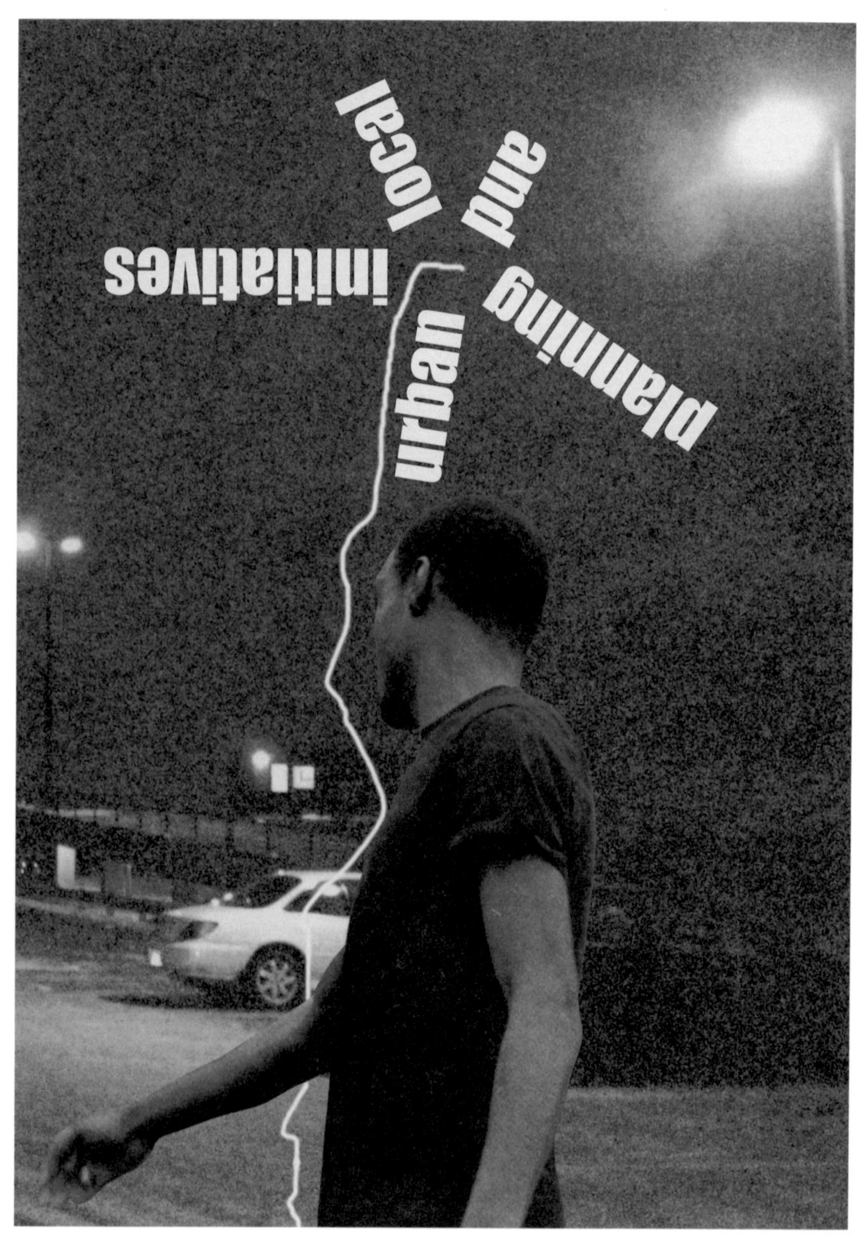

local
and
initiatives
urban
planning

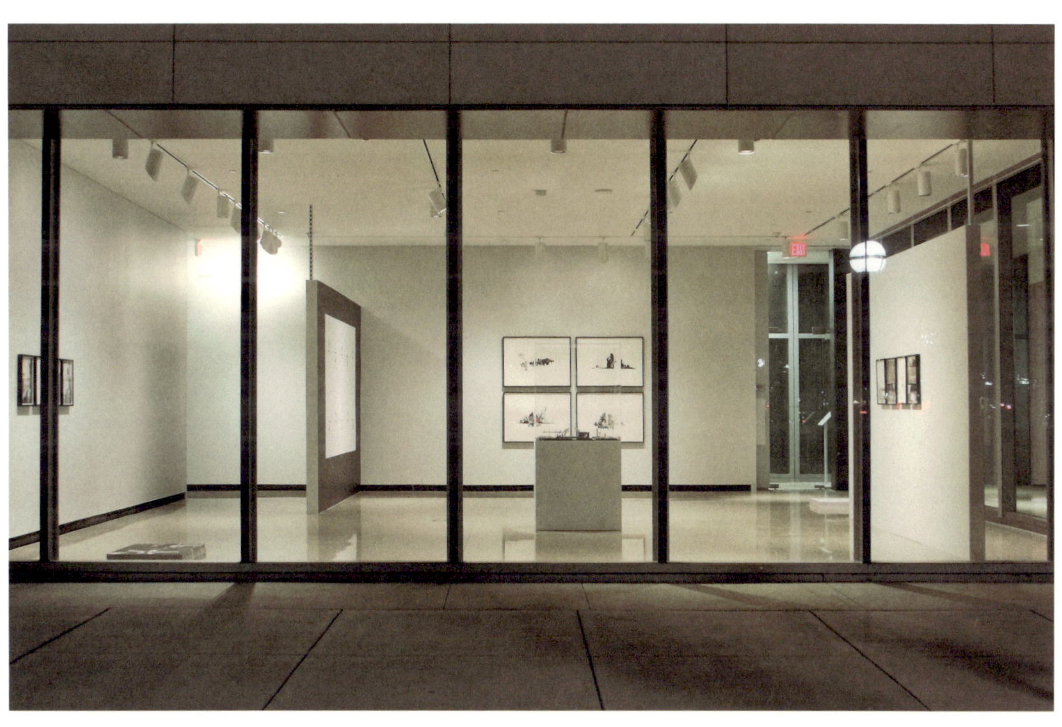

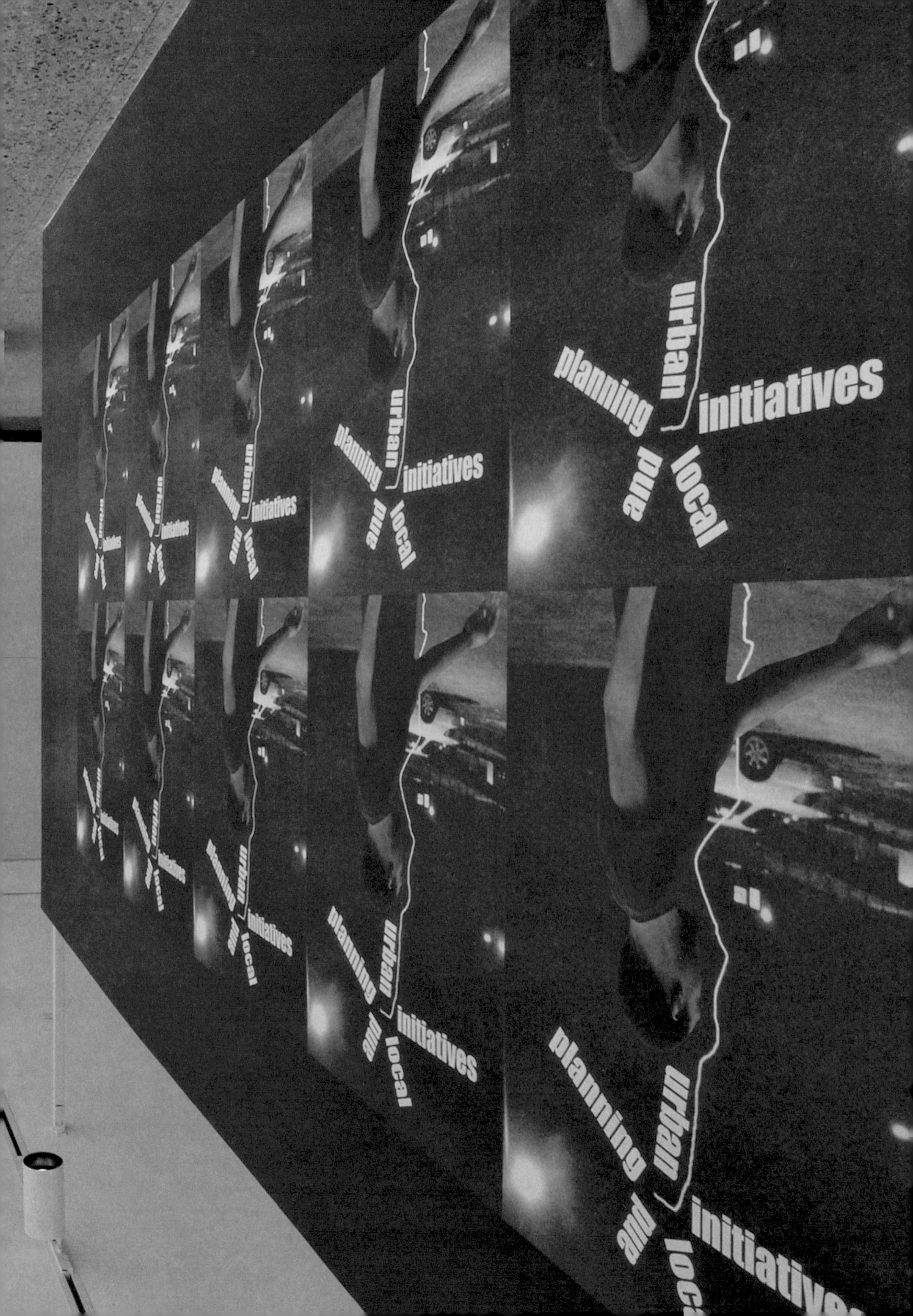

urban
planning initiatives
and local

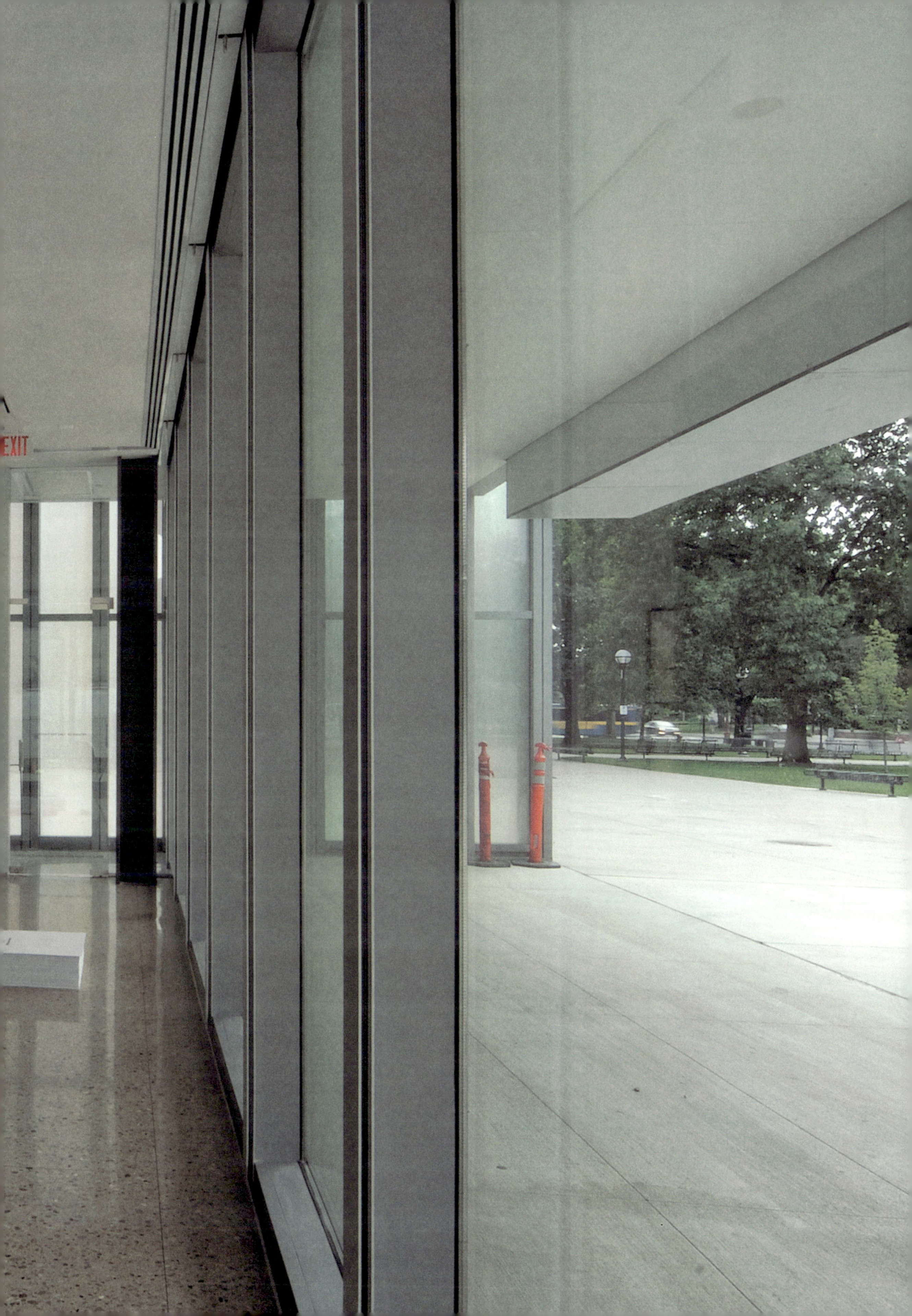

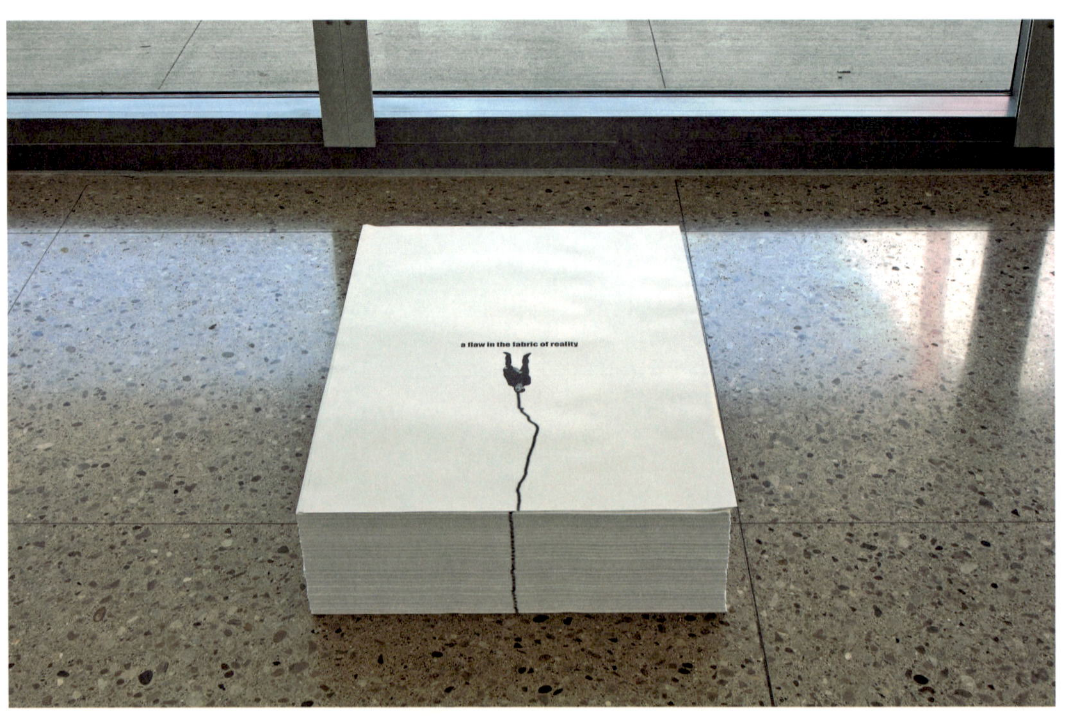
a flaw in the fabric of reality

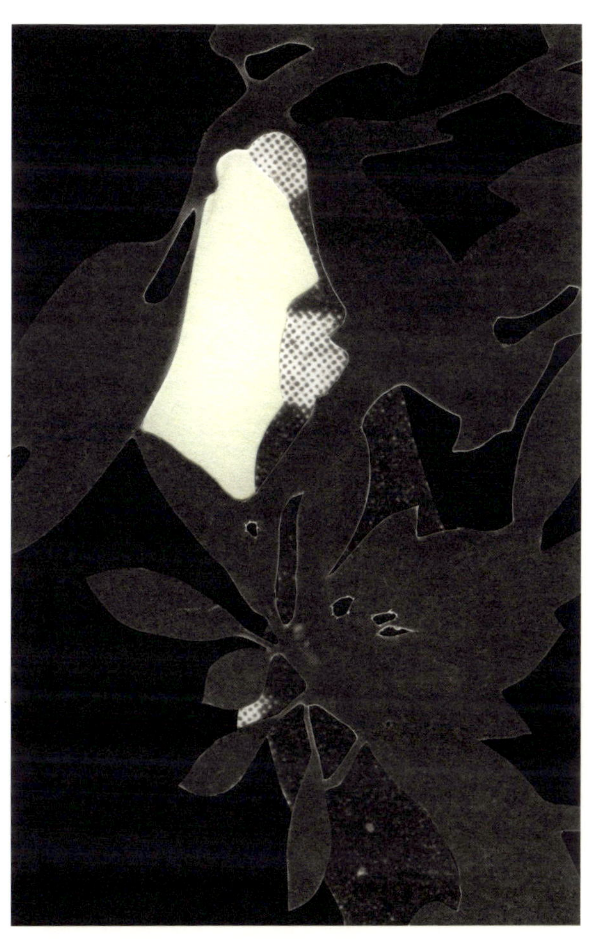

This book is published in conjunction with the exhibition:
UMMA Projects / Jakob Kolding
University of Michigan Museum of Art,
Maxine and Stuart Frankel and the Frankel
Family Wing, July 31 – October 24, 2010

University of Michigan Museum of Art
525 South State Street
Ann Arbor, MI 48109   USA
T +1 734 764 0395, F +1 734 764 3731
www.umma.umich.edu

Regents of the University of Michigan:
Julia Donovan Darlow, Ann Arbor
Laurence B. Deitch, Bingham Farms
Denise Ilitch, Bingham Farms
Olivia P. Maynard, Goodrich
Andrea Fischer Newman, Ann Arbor
Andrew C. Richner, Grosse Pointe Park
S. Martin Taylor, Grosse Pointe Farms
Katherine E. White, Ann Arbor
Mary Sue Coleman, ex officio

Exhibition curator: Jacob Proctor

The artist and the curator would like to
thank the following for their contributions
to this project:
Philipp Arnold, Eugenia Bell, Luis Croquer,
Elodie Evers, Galerie Martin Janda,
Christoph Keller, Lars Bang Larsen,
Stephanie Miller, Lori Mott, Joseph Rosa,
Ruth Slavin, Team Gallery, Susan
Thompson, Galleri Nicolai Wallner

The exhibition and publication are made
possible with the support of the Danish Arts
Council Committee for Visual Arts and
UMMA's New Visions Venture Fund, in-
cluding the Dr. Robert and Janet Miller Fund

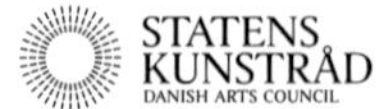

Christoph Keller Editions
Published in a limited print run, this series of artists' books and conceptual art publications,
edited and selected by Christoph Keller, aims to explore the bandwidth of artistic
book-making and the mediation of contemporary art in the printed format of the book.

Other titles in this series:
Emmanuelle Antille, *Tornadoes of My Heart*
Helen Mirra, *Cloud, the, 3*
Jonathan Meese & Slavoj Žižek, *Ernteschach dem Dämon*
Peter Piller, *Teilzeitkraft*
Mungo Thomson, *Negative Space*
Stuart Bailey & Ryan Gander, *Appendix Appendix*
Peter Piller, *Nijverdal/Hellendoorn*
Matias Faldbakken, *Not Made Visible*
Johannes Wohnseifer, *Werkverzeichnis, 1992–2007*
Archiv Peter Piller, *nimmt Schaden*
Mai-Thu Perret, *Land of Crystal*
Julien Berthier, *Nothing Special*
Archiv Peter Piller, *Zeitung*
Michael Stevenson, *Celebration at Persepolis*
Jonathan Monk, *Complete Ilford Works*
Zilla Leutenegger, *Zilla and the 7th Room*
Aglaia Konrad, *Desert Cities*
Jeanne Faust, *Outlandos*
Loris Gréaud, *Cellar Door*
Claudia & Julia Müller, *Habitus vs. Habitat: Primaten*
Boris Groys & Andro Wekua, *Wait to Wait*
Korpys/Löffler, *Die Sehnsucht nach Glück…*
Anna Lea Hucht, *Sprich mit Deiner Seele*
Jonathan Monk, *Studio Visit*
Yann Sérandour, *Inside the White Cube, Overprinted Edition*
Falke Pisano, *Figures of Speech*
Heidi Specker & Theo Deutinger, *Help Me, I'm Blind*
Philipp Lachenmann, *Some Scenic Views*
Ryan Gander, *Catalogue Raisonnable Vol. 1*

Published by: JRP|RINGIER
Letzigraben 134   CH-8047 Zurich
T +41 (0) 43 311 27 50, F +41 (0) 43 311 27 51
info@jrp-ringier.com, www.jrp-ringier.com

JRP|Ringier books are available internationally at selected bookstores and
the following distribution partners:

Switzerland: Buch 2000, www.ava.ch
France: Les presses du réel, www.lespressesdureel.com
Germany and Austria: Vice Versa Vertrieb, www.vice-versa-vertrieb.de
UK and other European countries: Cornerhouse Publications, www.cornerhouse.org/books
USA, Canada, Asia, and Australia: D.A.P./Distributed Art Publishers, www.artbook.com

For a list of our partner bookshops or for any general questions, please contact JRP|Ringier
directly at info@jrp-ringier.com, or visit our homepage www.jrp-ringier.com for further
information about our program

Jakob Kolding

Born 1971 in Albertslund, Denmark
Lives and works in Berlin

Select Solo Exhibitions

2010
UMMA Projects, University of Michigan Museum of Art,
Ann Arbor
Stakes is High, Stedelijk Museum Bureau Amsterdam

2009
Memories of the Future, Team Gallery, New York
Radical World, Studio Dabbeni, Lugano

2008
Posters, Fondazione Pastificio Cerere, Rome

2007
Overgaden – Institute of Contemporary Art, Copenhagen
The Suburban, Chicago
Rec, Berlin
Wall installation, Frankfurter Kunstverein bar

2006
Team Gallery, New York
Galerie Martin Janda, Vienna
Pattern Recognition, Marabouparken, Stockholm

2004
Space Invaders, Marres, Maastricht
Architextures, Fotogalleriet, Oslo
Spaced Out?, Museum in Progress and Arbeitskammer, Vienna

2003
Centre d'Edition Contemporaine, Geneva
Project with D.A.E., San Sebastian
Cubitt Gallery (with Luke Fowler), London

2002
Galerie Martin Janda, Vienna
Galleri Nicolai Wallner, Copenhagen

2001
Kunstverein in Hamburg
Projectroom, Finnish Photographic Museum, Helsinki

2000
Schnitt Ausstellungsraum, Cologne
Galleri Nicolai Wallner, Copenhagen

Select Group Exhibitions

2010
Museum of Contemporary Art Detroit
Polis Polis Potatismos, Malmö Konsthall
Kick-off, Kunsthallen Nikolaj, Copenhagen

2009
Fifty Fifty, Wien Museum, Vienna
You'll Never Walk Alone, Projekte SD, Barcelona
Reading the City, Limerick
Automatic Cities, Museum of Contemporary Art San Diego

2008
Home is The Place You Left, Trondheim Kunstmuseum
Games & Theory, South London Gallery
The Map is Not the Territory, Esbjerg Kunstmuseum
Moralische Fantasien, Kunstmuseum Thurgau, Ittingen

2007
Route A1, De Appel, Amsterdam
Habitat/Variations, Batiment d'Art Contemporaine, Geneva
Political/Poetical, Tallinn Art Hall
Differentiated Neighbourhoods of New Belgrade, project for the
Centre for Visual Culture of the Museum of Contemporary Art,
Belgrade

2006
For All Audiences, Sala Rekalde, Bilbao
The Urban Condition, Museum De Paviljoens, Almere
Skate Culture, Preus Museum, Horten
Ideal Cities/Invisible Cities, Zamosc and Potsdam
When the Moon Shines on the Moonshine, The Breeder, Athens
Busan Biennale
How to Build a Universe That Doesn't Fall Apart Two Days Later,
Wattis Institute for Contemporary Arts, San Francisco

2005
Social Democracy Revisited, Apexart, New York
Saltuna, Rooseum, Malmö
New II, Atelier Augarten, Vienna

2004
Public/Private - The 2nd Auckland Triennial
Platform, Istanbul
Wiener Linien, Wien Museum, Vienna

Posters, Videos and Other Stuff, Consulta/Santa Monica, Barcelona
Non Standard Cities, Schlachthof, Berlin

2003
GNS, Palais de Tokyo, Paris
Utopia Station, 50th Venice Biennale
Accessoiremaximalismus, Kunsthalle Kiel
Plunder, Dundee Contemporary Arts
Unbuilt Cities, Bonner Kunstverein, Bonn

2002
Concrete Garden, Museum of Modern Art, Oxford
Greyscale, Tramway, Glasgow
Mega Structures: Manifestos of Presumptuousness,
Vienna Architectural Triennial, Künsthaus Mürz
Centre of Attraction, Baltic Triennial of International Art, Vilnius
Rent-a-Bench, Los Angeles

2001
Take Off 20:01, Aarhus Kunstmuseum
Zero Gravity, Kunstverein Düsseldorf
Post Production, Arte Continua, San Gimignano
Intentional Communities, Rooseum, Malmö

2000
Organising Freedom, Moderna Museet, Stockholm
The Social Engineer, Transmission Gallery, Glasgow
Kwangju Biennale
Out Of Space, Kölnischer Kunstverein, Cologne
Momentum – The Nordic Biennial, Moss
Negotiations, Contemporary Art Center, Sète
Use Your Illusions, Part 3, Arnolfini, Bristol

1999
Bildung, Grazer Kunstverein, Graz

1998
Something is Rotten in the State of Denmark,
Museum Fridericianum, Kassel

1997
The Louisiana Exhibition, Louisiana Museum of Modern Art,
Humlebæk

· Luca Cerizza and Jakob Kolding, *Conversation Piece*, Newsletter
115 (Amsterdam: Stedelijk Museum Bureau Amsterdam, 2010)
· Paolo Antognoli, *A Town Called Alice*, Temporale 70 (2010)
· *Art and Text*, Aimee Selby, ed.
(London: Black Dog Publishing, 2009)
· *Utopics - Systems and landmarks*, Simon Lamunière, ed.
(Zürich: JRP Ringier, 2009)
· Robin Clarke, *Automatic Cities*, exh. cat.
(San Diego: Museum of Contemporary Art San Diego, 2009)
· *Beyond Architecture*, Lukas Feireiss, ed.
(Berlin: Die Gestalten Verlag, 2009)
· Andreas Nierhaus, *Fifty Fifty*, exh. cat.
(Vienna: Wien Museum, 2009)
· Jakob Kolding, *Border Communities*, Starship 11 (2008)
· Marco Scotoni, *Jakob Kolding, THE/END* (February 2008)
· Lars Bang Larsen, *Jakob Kolding at Overgaden, Artforum*
(October 2007)
· Paolo Antognoli, *Jakob Kolding – Collages and Urban Relation
Practices, Arte e Critica* (March 2007)
· Leire Vergara, *For All Audiences*, exh. cat.
(Bilbao: Sala Rekalde, 2006)
· Brigitte Huck, *Ideal cities/Invisible Cities*, exh. cat.
(Zamosc and Potsdam: European Art Projects, 2006)
· *22 interviews*, Thomas Trummer, ed.
(Vienna: Atelier Augarten, 2005)
· *Jakob Kolding: City 2* (Frankfurt: Revolver Verlag, 2004)
· Artwork for Lawrence *Remixes E.P.* (Dial records, 2004)
· *Jakob Kolding: Posters*
(Geneva: Centre d'Edition Contemporain, 2003)
· Xander Karskens, *CTRL-X – CTRL-V*
(Amsterdam: The Avant-garde Expectation, 2003)
· Petra Gördüren, *Accessoiremaximalismus*, exh. cat.
(Kiel: Kunsthalle Kiel, 2003)
· Artwork for Saint Etienne *Finisterre* album (Mantra Rec. 2002)
· Lars Bang Larsen, *Neighbourhood Threat, frieze* 66 (April 2002)
· Yilmaz Dziewior and Jörg Heiser, *Jakob Kolding*, exh. cat.
(Hamburg: Kunstverein in Hamburg, 2001)
· Jan Verwoert, *Zero Gravity*, exh. cat.
(Düsseldorf: Kunstverein für die Rheinlande und Westfalen, 2001)
· Astrid Wege, *Jakob Kolding - Schnitt Austellungsraum, Artforum*
(January 2001)
· Raimar Stange, *Der subURBANIST, Kunst-Bulletin* (March 2001)
· Will Bradley, *Park*, exh. cat. (Moss: Momentum, 2000)